DIPLOMAT IN WARPAINT:
Chief Alexander McGillivray of the Creeks

DIPLOMAT IN WARPAINT:

Chief Alexander McGillivray of the Creeks

by ARTHUR ORRMONT

illustrated with photographs

Abelard-Schuman
London   New York   Toronto

© Copyright 1967 by Arthur Orrmont
Library of Congress Catalogue Card Number: 67-18120

Standard Book No. 200.71516.X

First Published in Great Britain in 1968

London	*New York*	*Toronto*
Abelard-Schuman	Abelard-Schuman	Abelard-Schuman
Limited	Limited	Canadian Limited
8 King St. WC2	6 West 57th St.	896 Queen St. W.

Printed in the United States of America

"If ever there shall arise a weird pen fitted to deal with such a subject as Alexander McGillivray, it will find in this remarkable man's character and career a theme full of inspiration and demanding all its power . . ."

Absalom H. Chappell,
Miscellanies of Georgia

CONTENTS

ILLUSTRATIONS

AUTHOR'S NOTE

No picture of Alexander McGillivray appears among the photographs in this book. The reason is that none exists. Except for descriptions penned by his contemporaries, we would not know what he looked like.

Any biographer of Alexander McGillivray would be remiss in not expressing his indebtedness to John Walton Caughey, professor of history in the University of California at Los Angeles and pioneer biographer of the great Indian diplomat. In his able book, *McGillivray of the Creeks,* Professor Caughey has gathered together documents and source material without which this book could not have been written.

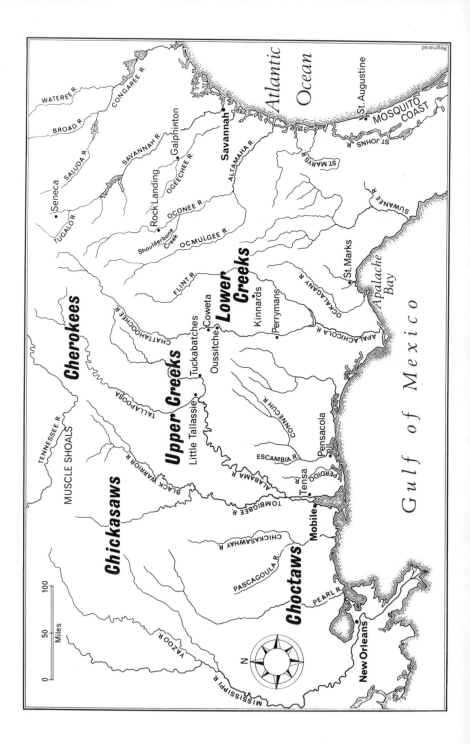

I

ON THE BANKS OF
THE COOSA

The group of Indian youths, most of them fourteen to sixteen years old, squatted or sat at the edge of the ball field, waiting their turn to play the game. They were naked, except for breechclouts and moccasins. Their racquets, or hurls, lay beside them. Some kept up an incessant chatter, commenting enviously or disparagingly on the athletic abilities of friends or acquaintances presently engaged in the contest. Perhaps the most vocal of these was a squat, powerfully built youth of eighteen, whose unflattering remarks seemed to amuse his listeners. Others of the group were silent, observing the game or biting on grass stems plucked from the field. Occasionally one slapped at a pestering gnat or insect.

Another youth, who sat a little apart from the others with his long-handled racquet on his knees, stood out from his companions by virtue of more than his physical distance from them. Whereas his companions' complexions were a deep olive, tending almost to copper, his was a light olive, tending to white. While most of his friends were robustly built, he was tall, spare and almost delicate in frame. He had long tapering fingers and his eyes were large, bright and penetrating. What was most noticeable about him was the peculiar shape of his forehead, which was considerably wider at the top of his head than at the temples. But this was not a disfiguring feature; the Creek maidens of Little Tallassie considered the tall youth to be an uncommonly handsome lad. Many wenches glanced at him boldly in the town square, and at the harvest dances he was much in demand as a partner.

One of the youths pointed to the field. "Look," he said. "It's Red Feather, he's hurt."

The tall youth got to his feet with the others to observe the crisis. Being carried off the field on a stretcher of rawhide always on hand for emergencies was a young Indian twisting and writhing with pain. The path that led to the town began where the group of waiting players stood, and in a moment the stretcher-bearers, running at a trot, had approached. The group parted to let them through.

The injured player had broken his leg. Below the knee the bone shone through the flesh, an obscene sliver of white against his dark skin. Although in terrible pain, Indian-like, he uttered no sound. Looking, the tall youth blanched, a reaction not shared by his companions, who, as the stretcher-bearers moved away down the path, laughed and joked about the incident.

One among them, the squat youth, had noticed the more sensitive boy's reaction. Swaggering up, he planted himself before him with hands on hips, contemptuously. The other youths gathered round. Although they were cousins, the antagonism between the two boys was well known. Temperamental opposites, they were always at loggerheads, although their elders had commented that it was always the older of the two, the heavily built youth, who provoked their quarrels.

"Cousin," he said now, "I saw you go white at the sight of a broken bone. Is this the way of a Creek warrior?"

The young lad replied quietly, "Cousin, neither of us will be Creek warriors until we have taken an enemy scalp."

The answer brought a flush to the face of the older boy and laughter from the others. Angry now, the squat Creek answered, "I say you will never take an enemy scalp, Choctaw or white. I say you are a woman, and afraid."

The younger boy moved an inch closer to his racquet on the ground. "Cousin," he said, "retract what you have said." To call a male Creek, young or old, a woman, was the ultimate insult of the tribe. Many combats to the death had been known to follow it.

"Why should I take it back?" the squat youth said belligerently. "When I know that you cannot stand the heat of the hothouse. That you show fear in a canoe on the water. That you wince when a child tortures a dog."

"I will not deny that I dislike the water," the tall boy replied. "Many of our great chiefs have shared that dislike with me. When the steam burns in the hothouse, I consider it foolish not to leave. As for cruelty to a defenseless animal, if you wish to praise it that is your affair." He paused at the mutter of disapproval this last remark had caused among his peers; it was difficult for a normal young Creek to believe that animal-baiting was anything more than an amusing sport. "I am waiting for you to retract your insult," he went on. "Either do so or move away. I do not like your odor."

The crowd laughed uneasily. To imply that a person smelled badly was an insult equivalent almost to questioning his masculinity.

The short boy's face mottled with rage. Deliberately he spat at his cousin's feet. Mimicking the other's calm, precise tone, he said, "Alexander McGillivray, I, Charles Weatherford, call you not a woman, but a young girl."

What happened then happened so quickly that the observers were powerless to prevent it. Alexander lunged for the long-handled racquet at his feet and, swinging it from the waist, struck Charles Weatherford on the side of the jaw. He dropped to the ground like a stone. The fight was over before it had begun.

Charles Weatherford's arrogance had made him few friends in Little Tallassie, but what Alex McGillivray had done was, by Creek standards, inexcusable. Challenged to a fight with fists and feet, he had used a deadly weapon. His cousin wasn't fatally injured; his labored breathing and a series of dull groans were evidence that he would gain consciousness momentarily. But young McGillivray had committed a crime—a crime that, had he been three or four years older than his sixteen years, and not descended from the aristocratic, privileged Wind Clan, surely would have resulted in severe punishment, perhaps even banishment from the community.

Threateningly the youths closed in on him, on their faces shock, rage and disgust.

Alex stood his ground. He did not raise his voice as he said, "No doubt many of you will wish to support Weatherford's charges against me. But I feel I was right. Now let me pass."

Perhaps it was the boy's dignity and assurance, or his social standing in the community, or the fact that he was the son of Lachlan McGillivray, the most important white trader in the Creek Nation. In any case, as he moved forward, the young men surrounding him fell away.

A moment later he was trotting down the path that led to Little Tallassie, and, a few miles beyond, to his father's plantation house at the bend of the Coosa River. No one followed to seize and take him into custody. But the boy knew that he was in serious trouble, and that the unpleasant aspects of the situation had only begun.

Lachlan McGillivray was an impressive man. Although not tall he was solidly built, and though now in his middle forties, he still had most of his flaming red hair, worn in the fashion of the time in a neat queue. His eyes were shrewd, his mouth resolute and his bearing erect. He looked every inch the successful trader and politician that he was. Even at Little Tallassie, in the heart of the central Alabama wilderness, he dressed as elegantly as though he were a Charles Town businessman with offices at the Exchange.

Today he wore a blue broadcloth coat and fawn knee breeches; his wrinkleless white silk stockings set off his well-shaped legs. Alex, sitting on the settle in the plantation house parlor, admired his ruffled satin shirt as Lachlan McGillivray strode up and down before him.

"But such impulsiveness, Alex—such reckless impulsiveness!" his father said, shaking his head. "I never thought you had that trait in ye!"

Alex could have reminded his father that impulsiveness was one of the few traits he had inherited from him. When only sixteen Lachlan McGillivray had run away from the home of his wealthy parents in Drumnaglas, Scotland, and shipped to Charles Town with only a crown left over from his fare. Instead, Alex merely repeated, for the fourth time, his reasons for striking Charles Weatherford with a deadly weapon. Charles was eighteen, two years his senior. He was at least twenty pounds heavier. It hadn't been just for Weatherford to challenge him to a "fair" fight. What chance would he have had against him?

"Ye've always been good with words," McGillivray said, "but that doesn't change the fact that you swung a hurl at Charles's head. You fought not as an Indian but as a white man would, a backwoodsman, taking the advantage and no holds barred."

"Is not Charles himself half white, and am I not three quarters, Father?" asked Alex quickly.

"Yes, but your mother is a Creek and you were born in the Creek Nation. You grew up in Little Tallassie, where even a full-blooded white must do as the Creeks do when in their midst."

Alex could have brought up in rebuttal his father's elegant dress and civilized way of life, but refrained; Lachlan McGillivray did not relish being told he was wrong. Yes, he thought, he had been born a Creek and was proud of it. The Creeks were the foremost Indians of the South—the most redoubtable in battle, the best farmers and craftsmen, the most favored in mental and physical endowment. But he, Alexander McGillivray, bore a white man's name and had white blood in his veins—half from his father's side and a quarter on his mother's, who had been half French. He had been educated as a white by a succession of white tutors— Scotch Presbyterians, French Catholics, English Church-of-Englanders. It had been his white blood and his white training, not cowardice, that had made him react as he had in the crisis with Charles. And surely it was also his white blood and training that made him detest such features of Indian life as the tortures of the hothouse and cruelty to animals. Why couldn't his father understand that?

"I've made a decision," Lachlan McGillivray said. "Ye've disgraced yourself here, and even if John Weatherford doesn't bring the matter up before the Council, one of these days his son is going to make it his business to kill or maim you. I want you to go to Charles Town, to study there with my brother Farquar. Ye'll leave with the first pack train out of Little Tallassie. *If* I can persuade your mother to let ye go."

Charles Town! To live and study there with the Reverend Farquar McGillivray! Alex's emotions at this moment were so confused that he couldn't begin to sort them out. It had been his dream to pursue his education in Charles Town or Savannah ever since he had learned to read. Only his mother's insistence that he wait till he was at least seventeen had kept him at Little Tallassie this long.

But he also had misgivings. How would he, who had traveled no farther than Augusta, Georgia, adjust in so civilized a city? And how would it be, living with the upright Reverend Farquar, who disapproved of his brother's marriage to an Indian "wench" and looked down upon him and his sisters Sophia and Jeannet as the unseemly issue of that union? Finally, his home and family had suddenly become very dear to him now that he was faced with losing them.

Lachlan McGillivray was not insensitive; he saw what emotions were tearing his son. He sat down beside him on the settle and put his hand on his knee.

He could imagine what Alex was thinking. It was hard to leave your home for a place you had never seen. And it was going to be no great fun living with his saintly brother. But Farquar was a good teacher, and Alex wouldn't be entirely alone—his servant Paro would go along and he could take his mare, Georgia. You couldn't be a gentleman in Charles Town without a servant and a horse.

Of course it wouldn't be easy persuading his strong-minded mother. Alex must pretend, and convincingly, that he'd like nothing better than to go to Charles Town to live with Farquar and his wife Amy and sweat over Latin and Greek.

Sehoy McGillivray was the daughter of Captain Marchand, who had once commanded Fort Toulouse, only a short distance from the McGillivray plantation. At the Hickory Ground, a few miles from the fort, young Lachlan McGillivray, just starting out as a trader in the Creek Nation, had met Captain Marchand's beautiful half-breed daughter, then sixteen. He promptly fell in love with the aristocratic girl, whose vivacity and slightly curling hair revealed her part-French ancestry.

The marriage, although frowned upon by his brother Farquar, had not only been a remarkably happy one but had done Lachlan no harm financially. By virtue of his connections with the powerful Wind Clan he was able to extend his projects and thus become a man of wealth, owning two plantations and numerous slaves, as well as stores and warehouses in Savannah and Augusta. With wealth had come power, and there was no political appointment in the western part of Georgia and central Alabama that Lachlan McGillivray had no hand in. Though a strong King's man he was on good terms with the less fanatical of the Whigs, who admired his shrewd farsightedness in siding alternately with both French and English interests as they best suited his own policy and fortunes.

Had Sehoy been an ordinary squaw she would have left business and politics to her husband. But she was not an ordinary squaw. She dressed in the highest Charles Town fashions and read the newest books; she also interested herself in her husband's affairs. Lachlan McGillivray had learned to trust her judgment in both politics and business, though, like other men of the times, he would have been disturbed had anyone but his closest friends known that his wife was anything more than an ornament to his dining room and parlor.

Now thirty-three, in this year of 1773, Sehoy McGillivray was a strikingly beautiful woman. Her white lawn dress dazzlingly set off her olive complexion and dark curling hair, on which a white lawn cap perched with just a hint of sauciness. Entering the parlor with his father, Alex once again marveled at his mother's beauty, a daily sight he would sorely miss.

Lachlan McGillivray had learned that in dealing with his wife he must come to the point quickly. Alex was glad to see that as his father spoke she never once paused in her sewing.

When her husband had finished she said to Alex, "Are you quite sure Charles isn't seriously injured?"

"If he had been, John Weatherford, your brother-in-law, would have been here within the hour," Lachlan McGillivray answered. "Of course I'll hear from him eventually. Probably before nightfall."

Sehoy nodded and looked at her son. She spoke somberly. There was an element here she said, that he and his father had evidently not considered. When she had been big with her son she had dreamed of great stacks of ink and paper, books and manuscripts. This had persuaded her that he would grow up to become a great statesman. One day he would, no doubt, wish to return to his people as a chief. That position was his by virtue of his descent from her clan. Should he leave now, under a cloud, it would be interpreted by the Creeks that he had voluntarily accepted banishment. If he returned soon this would be held against him by his fellow chiefs, and the obstacles to his rising to power in the Nation would be formidable.

"That is true," Lachlan said, "but Alex should be away at least four or five years. . . . Then you are agreeable, my dear?"

In answer Sehoy raised her arms to her son. Alex went into them, his eyes moist. "Alex," she said, "it's hard to lose you, but it is better that you go now. You are meant for the white man's towns and cities; what happened today has proved that. But it is very difficult for me to accept."

"Difficult for me too, Mother."

That could not have been more true. But at the back of his mind was another question that nagged him even more insistently. He had failed to conform to the world of the red man. He knew little or nothing of the white man's world. Would he be able to contend with it any better?

II

CHARLES TOWN

Had the Reverend Farquar McGillivray not married well he would have lived much less comfortably in Charles Town than he did; Presbyterian clergymen received small salaries. Fortunately his wife, the plain but pleasant daughter of an Ashley River plantation owner, had brought him a munificent dowry, and the McGillivray house on Legere Street, while no mansion, was one of the town's more attractive dwellings.

It was tall, narrow and made of brick with white woodwork and steps coming down to the brick sidewalk. The garden—Charles Town was a town of gardens—was on the south side, divided from the sidewalk by a brick wall and a wrought-iron gate. Behind the garden were the servants' quarters, the stables and the icehouse. The very simplicity of the place made it imposing. Anybody who passed by knew that the owners of such a house did not feel it necessary to prove they were financially comfortable.

Alex liked his room. It was more plainly furnished than his room at home and the mahogany bed and bureau had a Calvinist austerity about them typical of Uncle Farquar. The slop jar was devoid of ornamentation, as were his white pitcher and tooth mug. But there was a fireplace and plenty of closets, and the view from the window was magnificent.

Charles Town, built on a peninsula, lay spread out before him like a glistening jewel between two sparkling necklaces of water. At his left to the west, was the Ashley River, and on his right, the Cooper. Straight ahead, if distant, was the narrow neck of land joining Charles Town to the mainland. Behind him, where the two rivers met, was the sea.

Off to his right he could see the solid dark block of the Exchange, which was customhouse, post office and business center all in one. Under the Exchange, Uncle Farquar had told him, was the vault where lay locked up the first shipload of tea that had come bearing the King's tax. Uncle Farquar, a staunch King's man like his brother, strongly disapproved of the action, which he stigmatized as disrespectful to the Crown.

St. Michael's Episcopal Church on Meeting Street, with its tall spire, dominated the view. Distant in the bay were the tall masts of ships. In the narrow, cobblestoned street before St. Michael's stood the toga-clad statue of William Pitt that Alex had passed on his way to Legere Street. It had been put there, his uncle told him, to honor Pitt for persuading the British Parliament to repeal the Stamp Act.

Washed and changed from his traveling clothes to a respectable brown coat and knee breeches, with his next-to-best shoes and knee buckles, Alex went down to the parlor to join his uncle and aunt. The Negro maid, in neat blue homespun with a white cap and kerchief, was serving tea.

Amy McGillivray, dressed in a dark blue silk, its severity relieved by a white lawn cap on her greying hair, greeted him with her sweet smile. Farquar McGillivray put down his copy of the *South Carolina Gazette* and asked if he was pleased with his room.

"Yes, Uncle, especially with the view. Charles Town is so beautiful!"

"Indeed it is, perhaps too beautiful for its own good. Charles Town's atmosphere, so rich, sophisticated and old world, encourages its citizens to live at a giddy pace, on an ungodly scale. They overeat, they overdrink, and their morals . . . Well, you could do without a sermon with your first cup of Charles Town tea."

View of Charles Town before 1739

"I'm afraid Alex will get his sermon with his second," smiled Amy, and handed Alex his teacup and a buttered muffin. Alex accepted both with enthusiasm; he hadn't eaten since morning.

"And how is the family, Alex?" Amy asked. "Do you know I haven't seen your mother for almost four years now?"

"They are fine, Aunt. Sophia and Jeannet are growing up to be real beauties. They all send their love."

Amy nodded pleasantly, but an expression of disapprobation flitted over his uncle's wintry face. He would never approve of mixed marriages and the offspring thereof.

The Reverend put down his cup. "As you know, Alexander, your father sent me a draft that will cover all your expenses for at least a year. I think it best that we set a weekly allowance for you and in addition open up accounts

with a good tailor, haberdasher and other tradesmen. That way your bills will come directly to me."

Alex said this sounded fine.

"However, it brings up a painful subject that we had best discuss now."

"Farquar, do you really think . . ." broke in Amy Mc-Gillivray anxiously, but the Reverend silenced her with a ministerial glance.

"Charles Town," he continued, "is run by a well-to-do society of planters, merchants and lawyers. They are a snobbish lot who grovel at the superior culture and manners of England. Their sons are sent to Eton, Oxford and the Inner Temple; they disdain Charles Town College, founded three years ago by an excellent clergyman, Reverend Robert Smith. They also disdain anyone not of full white blood, not only

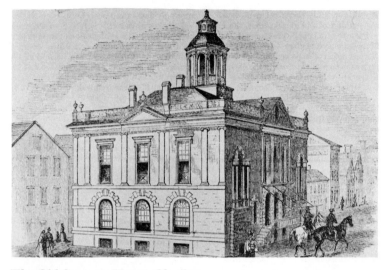

The Old Customs House, Charleston

because of their aristocratic notions, but because not so long ago Charles Town lived in terror of the Cherokee, the Choctaw and the Creek."

Alex's throat was suddenly dry, and he took a quick sip of tea.

"Now this snobbery and prejudice extends to that miserable species of creature that apes its betters, and these people are all too common behind the counters in the shops. They will take your money, Alexander, but they will also mock you behind your back. They will call you a mestizo, a halfbreed and worse."

"I see," said Alex, noticing that Amy's cup was rattling in her saucer. He loved her for being upset; it made him somewhat less so.

"The aristocratic young men of Charles Town," the Reverend went on implacably, "will not ask you as their guest to the horse races, the cocking mains or the Duck Street Theater. Nor will their sisters or their mothers invite you to tea." His tone softened. "Do not hate me for telling you this, Alexander. It hurts now, I know, but it would be much more painful later on were you not forewarned, and on your guard."

Alex had to respect his uncle for his frankness, especially since Farquar McGillivray was a snob himself, if a more sincere one than the kind with which Charles Town was evidently overrun. "I understand," he said, and though he was heartsick at the moment, his Indian blood stood him in good stead, for with a face that revealed nothing of his emotions, he asked his aunt for another muffin.

It was Aunt Amy who swiftly changed the subject, talking of points of interest in Charles Town that he must see tomorrow—the slave market on Chalmers Street, the Chamber of Commerce, St. Michael's, Solomon's Lodge No. 1, the first order of Ancient Free Masons in the colonies.

"Don't forget the Presbyterian Church," the Reverend put in drily, "of which I am privileged to be minister."

"Oh that too, Farquar," Amy said hastily, and she and Alex laughed.

The Reverend managed a smile. "Don't worry that I'll fill your brain with the glooms of Calvin," he assured his nephew. "You have an education, not a vocation, to pursue. There'll be Latin and Greek and French, when we have time for it. Also arithmetic, algebra and plane geometry. And English literature."

"History too, sir?" asked Alex hopefully. Just this year he had started reading in his father's library and had come across a book he particularly liked, a translation of Herodotus. He had read it at least three times and knew passages by heart.

There would be history, the Reverend Farquar said, but less history than English. He did not hold with the teachers of today that Latin was more important than English, and that a student of Latin would never have any difficulty in expressing himself in the mother tongue. The opposite too often was true.

Sully, the Negro maid, entered the parlor to say that Paro, Alex's servant, had groomed his horse, Georgia, for Alex's inspection. Alex excused himself and went through the garden to the stable. He was annoyed with himself for being so occupied with his own problems that Paro had slipped from his mind. Lachlan McGillivray had taught him that a master had no right to a servant unless he was willing to assume responsibility for him.

Paro, a young Negro perhaps eighteen years old—no one knew his real age—was waiting for him patiently. Georgia, Alex's black mare, stood munching oats; she had been beautifully combed and curried and looked none the worse for the hard five-day trip. Feeding her a sugar lump, Alex asked Paro how he liked his quarters.

"Dey fine, Master Alex. Clean and airy. I even got me a pitcher and a washbowl."

Alex asked Paro if he thought he would like it here in Charles Town. It was something of a delicate question, for in bringing Paro with him he had broken up a romance between the boy and one of the plantation housemaids. Paro replied with a grin that he thought he would. Sully had given him some milk and a hunk of cornbread without his even asking for it.

When Alex returned to the house Uncle Farquar was waiting for him. The Reverend suggested a stroll to the waterfront, and they set off for the bay area of the town.

The streets—it was now four o'clock—were full of people; he had never seen so many in his life. British soldiers sauntered up and down the brick sidewalks, doffing their tricorns to the shopgirls. Young ladies of fashion wearing silk mitts tripped along with dogs on leashes, their maids walking behind them. Colored women sat by the curbs, selling flowers. Ladies and gentlemen were making calls and soberly garbed

A typical 18th-century Charleston house

businessmen hurried home from the Exchange. A few elegantly dressed dandies stood in knots at street corners. One of them glanced at Alex's excellent-quality clothes and then at his face, his surprise unmistakable. He must be wondering, thought Alex, why a well-dressed Indian—or was it mestizo—happened to be out for a walk with a white clergyman.

The Reverend commented that the British soldiers stationed at Fort Johnson were none too popular with the townspeople, and Alex turned to his uncle with a look of interest. "Is that right, Uncle? Why?"

"I see that our difficulties with the Crown have not penetrated to your wilderness. We shall have to remedy that. Have you heard of the Townshend Acts?"

Alexander shook his head.

"The Townshend Acts of 1767 levied taxes on glass, painters' lead, paper and tea. Three years ago all duties except the tax on tea were repealed, but the principle of the right to tax the colonies was maintained. Do you know of the Boston Massacre?"

"Vaguely, sir."

"Lachlan must be so busy with backwoods politics and moneymaking that he does not inform his family of important developments in the world outside. I believe that we are headed for real difficulties with Britain. Already there are rumors that Sam Adams of Boston is working towards the calling of a Continental Congress."

"Is that bad, Uncle?"

As a King's man, the Reverend believed so. A Continental Congress could only lead to new explosions. At the same time he didn't deny that the Patriots, as the Whigs styled themselves, had much justice on their side. Taxation should involve representation, and the Crown had no right to demand that Americans pay for British troops quartered on them.

They were at the bay area now, and the smell of salt and tar was overpowering. Sailors hurried about, their wide breeches flapping about their knees. Soldiers in the King's red, relieved of guard duty in the harbor forts, were returning to the shore in rowboats. At the wharves the last of the rice, indigo and timber loads were being lowered into the holds of merchant vessels.

The Reverend said that Alex wasn't seeing the harbor at its best. For that he must get here early in the morning, when the docks were thronged with the women, white and colored, on their way to the fish stalls to get their choice of the morning catch, and the merchants going down to buy goods brought by the ships.

They started back up Tradd Street. At Meeting Street a wagon train blocked their path. Alex, who had seen many such trains set out from his father's warehouse at Little Tallassie, bound for Charles Town, Savannah and Augusta, watched a familiar sight. The horse-drawn trade wagons swayed and rocked as they clattered over the uneven cobbles. Their freight, he knew, consisted of deerskin, drums of beeswax, hands of tobacco, hemp and smoked meat. Lanky, leather-faced men in greasy hunting shirts walked alongside with their peculiar bent-kneed stride. Following the last wagon were Negro and Indian burdeners with packs on their backs. One of them, a wooden-faced Choctaw, by the looks of his flat head, stared impassively into Alex's eyes for a long moment, then turned away.

Alex felt strangely confused, even a little guilty, and didn't know why. It was a relief when he and the Reverend returned to the house on Legere Street and he could be by himself for a while. His first day in Charles Town had been a tiring one. He was plumb tuckered out, as the Georgia backwoodsmen put it.

Charles Town
May 12, 1775

Honored Parents:

I am sorry to have written so little lately, but will make a quick end of apologies.

I am sound and well, and trust you are the same. I hope you did not worry overmuch that I had caught the smallpox, which was active in Charles Town lately. However, I was fortunate and did not, although there were two families on Legere Street that suffered from it, and also their servants. At least forty persons died in the city.

It was thought for a while that Paro had come down with the pox, but it was only a fever that consumed him for three days, and then left as swiftly as it had come. The fever postponed his marriage to Sully, for which, Father, I am grateful for your permission, since it has made him happy. Now that they are man and wife this has necessitated some new arrangements in the servants' quarters. Aunt Amy presented the couple with a fine commode and I gave Paro a guinea as a wedding present.

This, Father, is the reason why I am a little short of money for the nonce, so if in your next draft to Uncle Farquar you will take note of it, I will be grateful.

I have had a letter from Sophia but none from Jeannet for some time now, and am sore at heart that she should thus neglect her brother. Will you tell her this for me?

Mother, you asked if I had grown and I am happy to tell you that I am now almost six feet in height, which is very tall for this city, especially compared to the Huguenot French, who are a tiny race. My life goes well enough and I am studying very hard; Uncle Farquar is a most exacting teacher. I am not overfond of Latin and Greek and like history best, and English literature. I am now reading Shakespeare's histories. Aunt Amy often comes down to the library at midnight to tell me I shall ruin my eyes unless I stop, and snuffs out the candles.

There is constant talk of politics in Charles Town. People were much disturbed at the news of Lexington and Uncle Farquar says that the loss of almost three hundred British regulars on the return from Concord is an earnest of coming war. The rabble, as you call it, Father, is coming out of its holes and there have been several instances lately of important persons, in their splendid coaches, being stoned by the mob. Last week the garrison at Fort Johnson was strengthened by another regiment of British foot.

I hope it will not disturb you, Father, who sympathize so strongly with the Crown in these disagreements, to know that my own opinions are not settled on the matter. There is much to be said for both sides. I know you will not hold this opinion against me, or feel that your decision to send me here was not a wise one.

Uncle Farquar said after services last Sunday that a Mr. Browning told him he visited you in Savannah last month, at which time you told him you expected to be in Charles Town on business before the fall. I hope Mr. Browning had accurate information.

My respects to you, honored Madam and Sir,

Your loving son Alex

This letter was only a partial reflection of Alex's current state of mind. It was not the practice or fashion of the day to bare one's soul in ink, nor did Alex's reserved nature permit him to bring up matters that would have pained his parents and made them worry for him. For, actually, he had withheld almost entirely the real truth about his life in Charles Town.

Not that he regretted having come here. In the almost two years that he had been studying with Uncle Farquar he had profited immensely. A whole new world had been revealed to him, and to plumb this world more thoroughly in the future would be a task he would never fail to follow with eagerness and delight. The life of the mind had been opened to him and he knew now that his greatest happiness would be to identify himself with that life and its disciplines. Not that he was a philosopher or had any talents in that direction; systematic or abstract thought did not interest him, as he had found from trying to read Aristotle and Plato. Rather it was men and events that occupied his mind, as they were seen in Plutarch, and the histories of a great genius like Shakespeare. Men influencing events and being influenced by them in turn; this was something that historians of the day seemed completely indifferent to, filling their books as they did with dates of wars and the accessions of kings. It was not the date that mattered, it was the man. The interests he represented, the interests he did not, and the reasons therefor. It was human passion, human desire and human greed that made history, and to know that was to begin to know human beings.

And how necessary it was for him to know men, their strengths and their weaknesses, in order to protect himself from them. For Uncle Farquar had been right in his warnings. In Charles Town, as a mixed-blood, a mestizo, he had become intimately acquainted with humiliation.

The approaching hostilities with England had much to do

with it. The Indian was still the colonists' most feared enemy. Everyone knew that the British, by their fair treatment of the Indian, had earned his loyalty. When war came, as it surely would, the Indians of the South—the Creek, the Cherokee, the Choctaw and the Chickasaw—would be the allies of England, nor would they miss this opportunity to drive the white settler from the lands they regarded rightfully as their own.

One afternoon he had stopped for a tankard of small beer at a tavern on Bay Street. At the next table sat two young men, from their appearance mechanics or laborers. They were flushed from heavy drinking.

"It's the Indians we got to fear, not the lobsterbacks," said the heavyset one of the pair. "At least the lobsterbacks don't scalp you."

"No, they'll skewer you with a bayonet," replied his thin, hawk-faced companion, who evidently had a wry turn to his wit.

The heavyset man continued earnestly: "You wouldn't talk that way, Jim, if your grandmother had been scalped by a murdering Cherokee. I tell you we've got to kill off the Injuns before war with the British starts. The British'll use them against us." He stopped as his companion, noticing Alex's presence, tapped him on the arm.

The heavyset man shifted in his chair to stare at Alex. His curious expression changed to one of outright hostility. "Well," he sneered, "here's an Injun dressed up like a regular gentleman. Look at the silk stockings. Where'd you steal them clothes, fellow?"

Alex paled, but said nothing. He had decided to finish his beer and leave the tavern as inconspicuously as possible. Several patrons had already interrupted their conversations to glance his way.

But the man, angered by his silence, lurched to his feet and approached the table. Leaning on it with both hands, he shoved his face close to Alex's. "Cat got your tongue, Mr. Injun? Why don't you answer me like a man?"

"I don't talk to pigs," Alex said, and grasped his tankard tightly by the handle. It would make a handy weapon. There flashed into his mind the time two years ago in Little Tallassie, when he had faced Charles Weatherford. Charles, though a half-breed himself, had disliked him for his white man's ways. Now he was facing trouble because a white man was hostile to the aquilinity of his nose, the coarseness of his hair, the olive tint of his skin.

"What did you say, Injun?" the man snarled.

"I said I don't talk to pigs," Alex repeated.

The man plunged across the table, hands reaching for Alex's throat. In one motion Alex rose and stepped aside. The table went over with a crash.

From nowhere the burly tavern keeper appeared to pinion the laborer's arms behind him and jerk him to his feet. Alex mopped beer suds from his short coat as the tavern keeper marched the laborer to the door and shoved him sprawling into the street. "Stay out of here, you rabble!" the publican shouted after him, and slammed the lower portion of the half-door shut.

Alex looked up to see the laborer's companion standing awkwardly before him. "I'm sorry," the man stammered. "I want to apologize for Jim. When he's in his cups . . ."

"I understand," Alex nodded, and gathering up the books he was on his way to return to the Charles Town Library Society, left the tavern. Though his face was expressionless, his heart was pounding. He was grateful for the longish walk to the Library Society and back to the house on Legere Street; it helped to calm him down.

There had been other incidents and episodes. The sniff and the disdainful head toss that had followed an initial glance of interest from a pretty young girl he passed on Broad Street one fine spring afternoon. The overpoliteness of an elegant haberdashery salesman who had sold him some shirts in an exclusive west end shop. The well-dressed planter's son whom he had sat next to in church one Sunday, and who, after a moment, had pointedly changed his seat. The mestizo fish seller in the market who had asked him, as a fellowman of mixed blood, to intercede with his American landlord to give him, the fish peddler, a better spot where he could earn a better penny.

The pattern was always the same. At first those who rejected him could not believe that there could exist in their midst an Indian who dressed like a white gentleman of the upper class. Then, having decided that he was a sport, and hence neither representative nor threatening, they either patronized him or contemptuously refused to admit his existence.

This was true only of the Americans, not the British. Never had an Englishman, by his attitude or actions, reminded Alex of his inferiority. Neither at his uncle's table, nor in the streets of Charles Town, nor in its places of business. The British were not provincial colonials but a sophisticated people. They had never fought the red man, except as the allies of the French in the French and Indian War. They had nothing to gain from his humiliation or his extinction. In fact the Englishman had courted the Indians' friendship as assiduously as the American had distrusted and spurned it.

These thoughts were to reoccur to Alexander McGillivray very often during his career. They were also to influence his conduct in the coming conflict between Britain and America, now looming ever more threateningly on the horizon.

III

THE STORM CLOUDS GATHER

Charles Town
July 18, 1775

Honored Parents:

No doubt by now you have heard the news of Bunker Hill. All Charles Town is agog with it and cannot understand how the vaunted British army could have sustained as many as one thousand casualties against a handful of colonials. They are also talking of General Washington's being named commander in chief; the Tories will not call him general, but mister. Uncle Farquar calls him mister, and I am sure that you, Father, do the same. There are rumors that the brilliant General Benedict Arnold will be conducting an expedition into the Maine wilderness against Montreal, but no one knows when he will start.

Charles Town is now politically a divided city. Many friends and families are separated over the words Loyalist or Patriot. Reverend Bullman of St. Michael's Church was unwise enough to preach a sermon criticizing the Secret Council, lately convened here, and the vestry acceded to popular demands for his dismissal. You can imagine how Uncle Farquar took the news. He avoids all political comment in his own sermons, although this means that Aunt Amy and I become recipients of the same at home.

I received a letter from Jeannet last month, but why does not Sophia write? Tell her that her brother is angry with her because he is perfectly sensible that she has the time and will send her no more presents from this civilized city unless she puts quill to paper in her brother's behalf.

Paro was ill with the flux this week but is now recovered. He and Sully are expecting a child towards the end of Fall. Georgia is in excellent condition and the envy of the young bloods hereabouts, one of whom approached me with an offer to buy her.

Last week I attended a cocking main through the kind offices of Colonel Stuart, who sends you both his respectful regards. I was fortunate to win two pounds betting on the white. The cocking mains here are as important as the races and are advertised months in advance. Recently the famous bay Flimnap outran the winner of the last sixteen races. I hear that over two thousand pounds changed hands in this race.

Uncle tells me my studies are coming along well although it appears I will never be a mathematician. It is history I like best. My French is fair and English literature good. My Greek and Latin are only passable, but I can quote Cicero better than I am given credit for.

Lately I have been telling Aunt Amy of Little Tallassie and the Creek way of life, in which she is very interested.

I read with interest, Father, in your last letter, of the esteem in which Charles Weatherford is held by the young braves, of whom he has become the leader although he has not yet taken a scalp in battle. When war comes, and if the Creeks honor their long-standing alliance with the British, he will have that opportunity and surely he will make the most of it. I will not envy him then as I do not envy him now; we cannot all be warriors.

Colonel Stuart tells me that he plans next month to visit Colonel Tait at Little Tallassie, at which time he hopes to pay his respects to you and Mother. He is grim-faced these days. Only recently a mob stoned his fine house and broke several windows. He advised me to leave Charles Town should British troops evacuate Fort Johnson, saying that in this case the mob would take over the city, and anyone who does not declare himself a Patriot will be thrown into jail. As the son of a man who has declared his loyalty to the King

I could not take that course, regardless of my own opinions. I do not wish to leave Charles Town, nor do I prefer to return to Little Tallassie just now. In the event that circumstances force me to leave here I ask for your permission to go to Savannah where Governor Wright is much respected, and continue my studies there.

My respects to you, honored Madam and Sir,

Your loving son Alex

Alex's letter was more casual than he felt; actually he was much concerned about the approaching conflict. His mother had already written that she wished him to return home, but Lachlan McGillivray believed full-scale war might be averted.

Alex's suggestion of Savannah, in the event that the British evacuated Charles Town, was a compromise which he hoped his father would accept. The Georgia city was a hundred miles from Charles Town and its troubles.

He did not want to go home until and when he absolutely had to. It was not that he thought of life in the wilderness with a shudder, or that, on the other hand, he was completely happy on the seaboard. Rather the truth was that he imagined himself dying of boredom without the stimulus of books and good conversation. If in that respect he had turned into a white man of cultivated tastes, so be it.

The letter was an early example of the diplomacy its writer was later to practice on a much larger and more portentous scale on behalf of the Creek Nation. Alexander knew it was impossible to hide the true state of affairs in Charles Town from Lachlan McGillivray; in any case, when Stuart visited Little Tallassie his father would hear of it. Admitting the truth, he lessened the possibility of its being used against him. At the same time he suggested an alternative, Savannah, enabling Lachlan to give in while saving parental face.

Aunt Amy was curious about the Creek way of life and

had many questions concerning Creek food, culture, manners and customs.

Alex told her of the Creek "thin drink," which tasted like rich sweet cream, made from the "milk" of pounded hickory nuts and pecans, mixed with oatmeal, sweetened with honey and flavored with the ashes of burnt straw. He told her about the rich meats of barbecued bear ribs and roast and stewed venison; of the delicious hot corncakes spread with nut milk and the roasted, honey-filled sour oranges.

He spoke of the Creek flair for design and color, and how it had produced the attractive one-story lodges and buildings so solidly built of cypress planks, roofed with cypress bark or shingles, whitewashed with ground oyster shells and decorated inside with colorful paintings of birds and animals. Most Indian houses consisted of four buildings set in a square. One was for cooking and dining, another was used for sleeping quarters, another as a storehouse for fruits and vegetables and the last as a corncrib. The Creek corncrib was so admired by the Georgian settlers that they had adopted it for their own.

Each square had a small kitchen garden. The communal field, where ball games were played, often between different towns, was some distance from the center of the town. In the large central square were the council house, a temple where religious objects were kept, a communal banquet hall and quarters for visiting guests. Before the council house stood a post painted either white or red.

All Creek towns were either red "war towns" or white "peace towns." In the white towns, sacred to peace, no war councils could be held or weapons stored or distributed. The white towns were a sanctuary to any man, white or red, saint or murderer, and no enemy could be killed within the limits of a town whose post was painted white. The red towns, near white or Indian enemies, had log fortresses with loopholes cut into the walls.

Alex spoke of the Creek religion, of the Good Spirit, called Hésakádum Esée, or the Master of Breath; and of the Bad Spirit, called Stefuts Aségó, signifying the devil. The Creeks believed that the Good Spirit occupied some distant, unknown region where game was plentiful and goods cheap, where the corn grew all year round, and the springs of water never dried up.

He told Amy of the Creek festivals, the most important of which, the Green Corn festival, or Busk, marked the beginning of the Creek New Year in August. At this time all fires were extinguished, all old clothing and furnishings burned, all lodges scrubbed clean, all debts canceled and enmities forgiven. As of the New Year, any unsatisfactory marriage could be annulled forthwith. The priest kindled the "new fire," from which all other family fires were lit. A period of fasting and purification through imbibing of the alcoholic-emetic "black drink" followed, which was followed in turn by eight days of feasting and dancing, accompanied by hand drums, cane flutes and gourd rattles.

Aunt Amy said she was shocked by the low estate of Creek women, whom Alex described as utterly subservient to the men, both in house and field, except for those aristocratic women of the leading clans. Single girls were called "wenches" and married women "bound wenches." They had no will of their own, except in the management of the children; they even lived apart from their husbands in a hut or cabin adjoining the family lodge. Amy was especially distressed by the Creek lack of romance, and the fact that the refined passion of love was unknown to them. The Creeks applied the word "love" to rum, blankets or anything else they wished to possess; if a woman happened to be desired by one of them he applied the word to her, too.

And as Alex told his aunt of the Creek customs, he felt at once nostalgic for home, and even further removed from it.

The storm clouds, steadily gathering, suddenly broke.

On September 15, 1775, Lord William Campbell, British governor of Carolina, fled Charles Town aboard the English man-of-war *Tamar,* taking the Royal Seal with him. Many thought his departure unduly delayed, for a Provincial Congress had already met in the city, authorized the issue of one million pounds for military defense, and appointed thirteen prominent Patriots as a Council of Safety with power to command all soldiers, use all public money in the province and enter arsenals and storehouses to seize British arms and ammunition.

Patriotic committees were formed to work together to interpret the regulations of the Provincial Congress, deal with any threats of slave uprisings and silence "foreign incendiaries," meaning Tories. Several of the city's leading Tories were tarred and feathered and carted through the streets before being exiled to the West Indies.

The Provincial Congress stood ready to expel all officers representing the King in South Carolina. However, most sympathizers with the Crown in Charles Town took heart from the congressional edict which stated that its purpose was to establish a regular government until an understanding with the Mother Country had been achieved.

One afternoon in early October Alexander returned home to find four Committee of Safety militiamen, under the command of a corporal, leading a white-faced Farquar McGillivray away. From a ground-floor window Aunt Amy watched, wringing her hands.

Though the Reverend signaled him not to interfere, Alex demanded to know the charge under which his uncle had been arrested. The corporal asked his name.

"Alexander McGillivray. The Reverend is my uncle."

"Well, as a fellow Scotsman, I'll tell ye. The Committee asked for all tools in Charles Town, and yer uncle here neglected to send his."

"That's a pretty trivial reason to arrest a man. How long do you plan to keep him in custody?"

"Till he gives up the tools. That's the ruling."

Alex turned to the Reverend. "Uncle, why not give up your tools now and avoid arrest?"

"I will be glad to," said the Reverend stiffly. "The corporal did not see fit to tell me I had that privilege."

"Will you release him, then, if I take you to the toolshed?" Alex asked the corporal, and the latter nodded. Fifteen minutes later the militia detail had left, laden down with the Reverend Farquar's tools.

Still shaky, the Reverend unbent to the extent of a brandy in the library. "That was good thinking, Alex. Thank you. I was so upset by the thought of jail that my wits were quite uncollectible."

"The situation's getting serious if the Committee can throw people in jail for forgetting all its absurd edicts."

"I didn't forget, I neglected to comply. But you are quite correct. Let it be a warning: Once the Committee finds out you're Lachlan McGillivray's son they may make an object lesson of you. I would leave Charles Town, and soon."

"No, Uncle, I'll take my chances here," said Alex stubbornly.

"You wouldn't enjoy the scent of tar or the feel of feathers," said the Reverend, downing the last of his brandy, "nor to be split apart on a sharp rail. I must tell you, Alex, that I have written Lachlan of the situation here and of my concern. Much as Amy and I would miss you, I considered it my duty. Please, my boy, do not be angry with me."

"I'm not angry, Uncle," Alex said, sighing, as he left the room.

Lachlan McGillivray did not appear in Charles Town to fetch his son home; probably he had decided that as long as his brother was at liberty Alexander was safe too, at least for the time being. But there was no doubt that the situation in Carolina was worsening steadily. That November several more prominent Loyalists of the city were banished to the Bahamas after confiscation of their property, and the *South Carolina Gazette*'s tone against "the maleficent Tories" took on a new stridency. Now any man seen wearing Tory green, by happenstance or design, took his chances of being set upon in broad daylight by hooligans and rowdies. The *Gazette* reported that a green coach had been stoned on Tradd Street and all its windows smashed, merely because of its color. The occupant had been a member of the Congress.

Early in the new year of 1776 Charles Town learned of a clash between the Virginia militia and the British at Great Bridge. The British commanding officer fell and the militia pursued his troops and took possession of Norfolk. The Charles Town Whigs celebrated a victory that was to be premature, for a short time later Norfolk was bombarded by a British fleet and reduced to ashes.

In February Lachlan McGillivray arrived to stay at Legere Street as his brother's guest. He met with prominent Tories, including the Indian Commissioner, John Stuart. Alex was fully prepared for the serious conversation they had on the second day of his father's visit.

"It's time you left here, Alex," Lachlan told him. "The talk is that next month, if not sooner, the Provincial Congress will set up a constitution with John Rutledge as President. Charles Town will prepare for war then in earnest, and it is well advised to do so, for a British fleet will be sent to take the town."

"Which of course they will succeed in doing?"

"One must never assume, as I have tried to teach you. In any case Charles Town will be no place for a son of mine."

"Let me go to Savannah, Father, as I've asked," Alex said. "Everybody agrees the British are too firmly entrenched there to be ousted permanently."

"Alex, in this crisis your place is with your family, at home."

"Then you forbid me to go to Savannah?"

Lachlan smiled. "I would not be that foolish; you would come to hate me for it. I will merely refuse to contribute to your support in Savannah. You would have to give up Paro and Georgia, and a gentleman's life. In short you would be obliged to underwrite your decision, abandon your education and go to work. And do not expect me to find a position for you."

"In other words, if I cannot maintain myself in Savannah I'll be *forced* to return home?"

"I am offering you a compromise, Alex. You must compromise, too."

Alex asked when his father intended to discontinue his allowance.

"At the end of next month. You will need funds to get settled in Savannah."

In the space of a minute he had lost his status as a gentleman and descended to the middle-class. A clerkship in a countinghouse, that was all he could hope for. For a moment his courage fled. Then, as he saw Lachlan studying him, he knew that he could never allow himself to lose this first real battle with his father. "Thank you," he said, and got to his feet.

Lachlan McGillivray's shrewd eyes followed his departing son with regret and admiration. He knew the boy existed no longer; Alex had come to a man's estate.

IV

SAVANNAH, 1776

Savannah, birthplace of the Georgia Colony, was built on a walled bluff overlooking the Savannah River. Encircled by pine woods and set amid dark moss-curtained live oaks, it was only sixteen miles from the Atlantic Ocean, hence the faint tang of salt winds that braced Savannahites as they walked through the town.

James Oglethorpe founded Savannah in 1733 and gave it its name, derived from the Shawnee Indians who had once inhabited the river valley. Protestant groups from Europe and wealthy men had helped to give the colony a cosmopolitan population. After the attempted cultivation of silk, wine and medicinal herbs had failed, Georgia colonists had produced more practical commodities, and had developed a lively trade with England. In 1744 Savannah's first commercial house was established and soon afterwards regular export shipments of rice, hides and lumber were sent to the mother country. Five years later slavery was introduced.

In 1754 Georgia became a Royal province, and Savannah was named the seat of colony government. Two decades of commercial growth and improved trading conditions followed. The town had many wealthy Loyalists, men perfectly satisfied with the way Britain had lined their pockets; still, there was a strong Patriot element that had shouted approval of the Lexington victory, set up a liberty pole before Tondee's Tavern and organized a battalion of infantry commanded by Colonel Lachlan McIntosh.

In January, 1776, British war vessels anchored off Tybee Island and the Royal Governor, Sir James Wright, escaped on one of them to Halifax. Savannah was in Patriot hands.

But the town was poorly defended, and it was generally agreed that the British could retake it with little trouble whenever they wished. Under the circumstances the Loyalists were tolerated, and met with little persecution; the Patriots wished to avoid Loyalist revenge when and if the British chose to resume occupation.

Alex arrived in Savannah in early April, a short time after South Carolina had inaugurated a new government with John Rutledge as President. After finding lodgings on Bull Street, which formed the central axis of the city, he presented himself at the countinghouse of Samuel Elbert, a Savannah merchant whose name he had heard in Lachlan McGillivray's conversation over the years.

Elbert was a red-faced choleric man who was obviously annoyed that his routine had been interrupted by a stranger.

"McGillivray, eh?" he asked and paused. "Could you be related to Lachlan McGillivray of Georgia and Alabama?"

"I am his son, sir."

A more cordial look came over Mr. Elbert's face. "Well, give him my compliments. Do you come on business from your father?"

"No, sir, without his knowledge." Alex took a deep breath. "I have come to ask you for employment."

"Employment? Surely you could find employment with Lachlan? I don't understand."

"My father wants me to return home. I do not wish to. We have compromised on the basis that I live and work in Savannah."

"Ah, I see. Your politics differ from your father's. Well, Alexander, let me tell you that I am a Patriot, and much as I respect Lachlan McGillivray as a businessman, I regret his allegiance to the Crown. It will end in his ruin. Yes, I think we can find a place for you here, that is, if you can read, cipher and add a column of figures."

"Yes, sir, I can, and my penmanship is excellent." He had

no intention of correcting Samuel Elbert's misapprehension about his own politics, if the result was a position for him.

"I can offer you two pounds, five shillings a week to start."

"I accept, sir." The salary was disappointing, but he would make do.

"Very well. You will start tomorrow. Are you satisfactorily settled here in town?"

Alex told him he was and, nodding, Mr. Elbert saw him to the door. Returning to his lodging house in fairly good spirits, Alex sat down and wrote his parents.

Savannah
April 7, 1776

Honored Parents:

I have a position with a Mr. Samuel Elbert, merchant of this city. In our conversation, Father, he spoke of you with much respect.

I am staying at a boardinghouse on Bull Street, whose location is pretty near the center of things. The house is run by a Mrs. Howard, the widow of a lawyer. She is of middle age and pleasant. My room is commodious if not elegant, and faces the garden.

At the moment there is only one boarder in addition to myself, a foppish young gentleman, belonging to one of Augusta's finest families, who has been exiled here for his propensity for drink and cards. He has a fine horse stabled nearby but no servant. Evidently his family wishes him to disgrace them elsewhere than in Augusta. We have met on the stairs and exchanged salutations.

Since you, Mother, are not too familiar with Savannah I will describe it to you. Along Bull Street are five squares that were originally designed as a defense against Spanish invasion. The Episcopal Church, also on Bull Street, is a handsome edifice although it in no way compares with St. Michael's. In the city market housewives patronize a horsecar that is driven into the market where purchases are made from the car windows. Most of the houses are built in the Georgian style. Usually they are three or four stories including a raised basement and stairs ascending to a high stoop. Most are made of the famous Savannah grey brick.

The atmosphere here is less strained politically than in Charles Town. If revolt comes at all it will come late. Georgia has been kindly treated by England, and Sir James Wright is missed by many since he departed a short time ago. The colony, furthermore, is isolated from the center of dissension and revolt to the north.

Although I miss Uncle Farquar's instruction already, I feel confident that my self-instruction in the evenings will be profitable. I have all my books in my room, which Mrs. Howard calls "the library."

Tell Jeannet and Sophia to write or I will send them no pretties.

Your loving son Alex

Revolt came to Georgia a bit sooner than Alex had expected. News of the signing of the Declaration reached Savannah on the afternoon of August 10. Alex at the time was enjoying an after hours ale with Jack Williams, a fellow clerk, at Eppinger's Tavern.

It began with a commotion in the street outside, and then a man, somewhat the worse for rum, burst into the tavern shouting, "They signed it in Philadelphia! The Declaration of Independence! We're free!"

Some customers stood solemnly to toast the new nation; others, including Alex and Jack, ran into the street to see what was going on.

A group of flushed-faced young men were erecting a streamered liberty pole in front of Eppinger's Tavern.

A view of Savannah, around 1778

Around them stood perhaps fifty citizens of Savannah, urging their efforts on. The ground was packed hard and it was difficult to dig a hole.

"Miles Eppinger won't like this," Jack Williams said, and Alex nodded—everybody in Savannah knew the tavern owner was a rock-ribbed Tory.

In another moment Eppinger, a barrel-chested German with a surly face, appeared on the scene. Pushing his way through the crowd, he confronted the Patriot leader, who had just handed his pick to an associate and was mopping his brow.

"You go and pudd dis ting up somewhere else!" shouted Eppinger.

The leader motioned the pick-wielder to continue. "What's the matter, Miles," he asked sarcastically, "haven't you heard the news? We're free, man, free!"

A yell of approval went up from the crowd, and one or

A typical 18th-century Savannah house

two threateningly shook fists at the German. Alex had to
admire Eppinger's bullheaded courage. Not only did he stand
his ground unflinchingly, but when the liberty pole was
finally set into the ground he plodded forward to remove it.

The Patriots leapt upon the burly German. One moment
he was erect, swinging his hamlike hands against his attack-
ers; the next he was down, with Patriots swarming over him.

As Alex moved instinctively to come to the man's aid, Jack
Williams grabbed his arm. "Don't, Alex! They'll kill you!"

Alex shook him off and waded into the melee. A back-handed blow caught him in the face and knocked him down, but in a moment he was up again and yelling, "Stop, you cowards! You're fifty against one! Give the man a chance!"

He might have been shouting in the wilderness for all the effect his words had. The Liberty Boys continued to beat Miles Eppinger until the tavern owner was near unconsciousness. Then, hauling him to his feet, they dumped him on the tavern threshold to the ministrations of his hysterical wife, and departed for other celebrations, leaving the liberty pole wobblingly in place.

Miles Eppinger was in bad shape. With the help of two slaveys, Alex and Jack carried him upstairs to the couple's living quarters and put him on the bed. One of the slaveys went to fetch a physician.

"We'd better go now," Jack said nervously. "If Mr. Elbert hears we helped a Tory he'll discharge us."

"We helped a human being, Jack. I would have done as much for any Patriot set upon by a Loyalist mob."

Eppinger, the doctor said, was badly hurt but had suffered no permanent injuries. He would be on his feet again after a rest of a week or so.

On the way home Alex saw that Savannah had given itself up to celebration. Tondee's Tavern was jammed with merry-makers. The city slept little that night. Citizens cheered when a great procession streamed by, a mock funeral cortege with the effigy of King George III in the coffin. There was a formal burial ceremony. English royalty and its leading symbol were no longer sacred in the colony.

It was mid-September before Alex could persuade Samuel Elbert to give him a few days off for a visit to Charles Town. Elbert wasn't exactly dissatisfied with his work, but on several occasions he had caught Alex reading history during slow periods at the countinghouse, and, in the opinion of the

Savannah merchant, Alexander McGillivray was not among the most dedicated of his employees.

Alex arrived in Charles Town in sweltering heat. There was a different atmosphere in the city due to its victory over the British under Clinton and Parker in June; people seemed to be breathing easier, and the tension he had felt last March, when a British attack was expected momentarily, had lifted.

Certainly Charles Townites deserved much credit for the brilliant victory won at Fort Sullivan. Seven newly organized regiments, never before under fire, had beaten off seven regiments of regulars and eight ships-of-war whose guns outnumbered by six-to-one the armament of Fort Sullivan. The British had been so badly defeated that it was doubtful they would launch another southern campaign for some time.

Uncle Farquar wasn't at all pleased by the American victory. It had, he said, given the rabble of the town an opportunity to persecute those loyal to the King. Three of his friends were languishing in jail, their only crime loyalty to the Crown. An act had been passed by the South Carolina Congress confiscating the estates of "insurgents and disturbers of the public peace," a convenient umbrella to catch the innocent. Other southern states had already begun the confiscation of Loyalist property.

"Fortunately this isn't true of Georgia—yet," his uncle told Alex. "Otherwise Lachlan would face the loss of his entire fortune."

This was a new piece of bad news. What if his father's property were confiscated and the Americans won the war? He, his father's heir, would be literally dispossessed, without a penny to his name.

His two days in Charles Town were all too brief. So too were to be his days in Savannah. A short time after his return he was discharged from Samuel Elbert's countinghouse.

For some time the merchant, without success, had been trying to engage him in political discussion, and evidently

Elbert had come to suspect that his sympathies did not lie wholly with the Patriots. Whether or not he heard about his aiding Miles Eppinger Alex never knew, but in any event Elbert called him into his office and charged that he had misrepresented himself to him as a Whig.

"You are wrong, sir," Alex told him. "You merely assumed I was a Whig because I did not use my father's influence to get myself a position."

"And you did not correct my misapprehension."

"Of that I am guilty."

Elbert stared at him coldly. "Exactly where do you stand, sir?"

"I am neutral."

"Neutral?" Elbert snorted contemptuously. "What does that mean? You are either a Patriot or a Tory, unless, like your father, you have interests to protect."

"I have interests to protect. Those of my people, the Creeks. You will not deny that the purpose of the American frontiersman has been, and increasingly will be, to drive the tribes from their hunting grounds and lands. If that is the case, how could I be for the Americans? I would logically be on the side of the British, whose purpose in America is commerce, not settlement and expansion. And yet I am not for the British, either."

"Why not?" asked Elbert sharply.

"Because I see myself, because of my Indian blood, as part red man, and because of my white blood, as part American. Not as a Scotsman, or a Frenchman, though I have French blood too, or as a Briton. I was born, after all, in America, like yourself."

"Very clever," said the merchant. "I might add, Mr. Mc-Gillivray, that you are cleverer with words than you are with figures. You made two mistakes in yesterday's accounts. And I am confounded sick of your reading at your desk. I have decided to give you notice."

"For my reading or my politics, sir?" asked Alex.

"For both. Good-day."

A few hours later a slave boy delivered a note to Mrs. Howard's. Lachlan McGillivray was at Tondee's Tavern and would expect his son for dinner at eight o'clock.

His father had engaged a private dining room. Alex twitted him about dining at the hotbed of the Savannah Revolutionaries—the Sons of Liberty met in Peter Tondee's long room to hatch their plots. Lachlan replied smilingly, "Good food has no politics."

He laughed when Alex reported his conversation with Elbert. "I never did like the prig, and he was sure to let you go when he discovered you didn't share his prejudices. It's clear you weren't cut out to be a clerk, and nothing's lost. You can come home now." He paused. "Now that you're almost twenty, it's time you took your rightful place in the Nation."

Alex had to agree. Elbert would see to it that no one else hired him in Savannah. He had no choice now but to pay his laundress and tell Mrs. Howard he was leaving.

Lachlan ordered another bottle of Madeira to celebrate his son's homecoming. Alex drained it with him, in fairly good spirits. If he had failed in Savannah it was through no fault of his own; honor had dictated that he not hide his true feelings indefinitely from his employer. And at the moment he didn't regret leaving civilization for Alabama. There were worse places than the forest with its pure air and clear streams. And perhaps, with a war on, Little Tallassie wouldn't be all that boring.

V

A CHIEF IN THE
COUNCIL HOUSE

Little Tallassie was much the same as when he had left it, a typical Creek village with lodges built around a square in which the old men lounged from sunup to sundown, gossiping and wrangling. Nor had the plantation, a few miles upriver, changed very much in his absence, although it was larger now with the addition of a new el to the mansion house, and an increase in the number of his father's slaves which had necessitated the building of a dozen new cabins in the Negro compound.

What surprised Alex was how his sisters Sophia and Jeannet had grown. When he left they had been sticks of girls; now they were handsome young ladies, almost as beautiful, in their dark-eyed, lissome way, as his regal mother. Sophia was seventeen, Jeannet fifteen. Even in the wilderness such good-looking girls did not have too much trouble finding suitors: Colonel Tait, the British agent, was paying court to Sophia, although Lachlan McGillivray frowned on his suit; the Englishman was at least twenty years her senior.

Alex was glad to be back, although he missed the amenities of seaboard living; he had so thoroughly identified himself with the white world that the sight of a naked Indian child playing in the mud before its parents' lodge, or torturing a dog, was shocking. And he had nothing in common with the illiterate braves of his own age who could talk of nothing but hunting and scalps. They looked with wonder at the books he carried under his arm and with contempt at his white man's breeches, still considered effeminate in the Creek Na-

tion. The incident on the ball field that had sent him to
Charles Town had been forgotten by the elders of the town,
but not by Charles Weatherford who was still his enemy. In
his cunning way Charles managed to embarrass him by issu-
ing invitations, in public, for hunting and scouting parties in
which he knew Alex had absolutely no interest. His refusals
were taken by the braves as evidence of unmanliness, exactly
the reaction that Weatherford had hoped to provoke.

There were other disadvantages to living in Little Tallassie. Had he not brought a trunkful of books back with him
from the civilized world he would have been at loose ends
entirely; he had gone through his father's library and the
only interesting person to talk to in the area, besides his
parents, was Colonel Tait. He was already awaiting the
irregular delivery of the *South Carolina Gazette,* with its
news of the outside world, like a shipwrecked mariner who
scans the horizon hourly for sign of a sail.

At the same time it was a comfort being in the bosom of
a family who cared for him and was concerned with his
welfare. And in Little Tallassie, as the son of Sehoy, a
Princess of the tribe's leading clan, and of Lachlan McGillivray, the nation's most important trader, he himself was an
important person.

At the end of his first week at home Colonel Tait called
with the war news. Word had just been received that the
American retaliation against the Cherokee towns, which
last June had risen against the frontiersmen of South Carolina, North Carolina and Virginia, had been completely
successful. All Cherokee settlements west of the Appalachians
had been destroyed, and neither their crops nor their cattle
had survived. Undoubtedly, Tait said, the Cherokees would
now be forced to take refuge with the Creeks.

Lachlan McGillivray snorted contemptuously. "Stuart and
Cameron," he said, referring to the British agents who had
convinced the Cherokee to rise against the Americans,

"showed very poor judgment and generalship. There were no British troops to back them up, which accordingly left the Americans unhampered and free to deal with the Indians. Had the rising been put off until a British army was in Georgia, it might well have proved successful."

"I agree," said Colonel Tait with a smile. "Charles Weatherford agrees also. An American bullet creased his gorget." Weatherford had been part of a handful of Creeks and Tories who had joined forces with the Overhill, or Lower, Cherokee tribes.

"Yes, and with all due respects to your mission here," McGillivray senior addressed Tait, "I hope the Creeks remain as neutral as possible in this conflict. The Creek can have no success against the Americans until the British invade the southern states in force. I am in complete agreement with the chiefs who prefer good sense to suicidal valor. They will be justified at the peace table, when the Cherokee are told what lands they must cede in payment for their folly."

"There is another way of keeping the Americans at bay in advance of another British campaign," said Tait. "That is the formation of bands of partisan Tories. A group of Rangers has been formed by the McGirth brothers in Florida to attack the Georgia border. Tory strength is great in all the southern states, and there is no reason why some very formidable guerrilla units cannot be formed in the Carolinas, Georgia and Alabama." The colonel turned to Alexander. "Would you be interested in a commission in such a force, Alex?"

"My sentiments are still neutral, Colonel. Nor, if they were not, would I, unlike Charles Weatherford, have any ability as a warrior to offer. But let me ask you a question that bears on the formation of a partisan Tory force: Would you admit that the backwoods Tories are in large part a pretty unsavory lot—outlaws, murderers and horse thieves who have fled the seaboard?"

"There are many vicious men on the Patriot side, too," Tait said. "But I will admit the truth of what you say."

"We both know," continued Alex, "that jealousies in the backwoods have produced many long-standing and bitter feuds. Since the war began rival families have chosen opposite sides, not because of politics but because of sheer vindictiveness and hatred of one another. This being so, would not the formation of bands of Loyalist guerrillas do the King's cause more harm than good? Because it would become a conflict between the law-abiding, the Patriots and the lawless, the Tories. And the hatred it engendered against the Tories would inevitably be directed against the King. Not only that—after the war the Tories would have to live with the hatred of the Americans against whom they had marauded, killed and fought."

Tait nodded. "Your logic is both interesting and impeccable, Alex, and I would say I am convinced by it were it not for the fact that it is not the lack of animosity among your enemies that wins a war, but military victory." The colonel laughed. "Let me say that with your subtlety of mind you would make a fine staff officer. If you wish, I will be glad to recommend you as such to the first British general who dares to set foot in the South!"

In the next weeks exhausted refugee Cherokees straggled steadily into the Creek towns, fifty or sixty of them asking the chiefs of Little Tallassie for asylum. They were given food to continue on their journey to the Choctaw tribes to the southwest, but the elders steadfastly refused them asylum or military aid, replying that they had plucked the thorn of warfare from their foot and that the Cherokee was welcome to keep it.

The Cherokee had been so manhandled that for some time they would be unable to defend themselves as a Nation. The Anglo-American settlers to the north of the Creeks would not lose this opportunity to make themselves so strong in the interval that when the struggle was renewed they would have little trouble holding their own.

The dispossessed, demoralized Cherokee made a profound impression on Alexander. They had not always been the defeated. Only seventeen years ago, in 1760, they had waged fierce war with the whites and beaten them badly, ravaging the Carolina borders, capturing British forts and successfully withstanding British armies. But although they had held their own in the field it had been at the cost of severe losses, and their long wars with the Chickasaws and Creeks had drained them further. As a result they had declined steadily in power and numbers.

The Cherokee defeat should serve as an object lesson to the Creek Nation.

In the next months Alex found himself becoming intensely interested in the question of Indian participation in the Revolution. What were the interests of the southern Indians in the war between the British and the Watcina, the Americans? What were the interests of the Creek Nation? Should the Creeks ally themselves with the British or assume a neutral posture, letting the white men fight it out between themselves?

To achieve any perspective on these questions one had to go back many years to the first meeting of the white man and the southern Indian. In the early part of the sixteenth century Spanish explorers sailing along the Gulf shore had come in contact with the coastal Indians. But it was not until 1540, when Hernando de Soto and his men, searching for gold, began their march inland that the Spanish met the tribes of the Lower Creek and passed through the towns of the Upper Creek in the region between the Coosa and the Tallapoosa rivers.

There were two differing traditions as to the origin of the Creek people. The first of these had their original seat in northern Mexico. The Creeks were said to have been a warlike and independent tribe lacking the comparative civilization of the Aztecs and the Tlascalans. Confederates of the latter in conflict with the former, the Creeks had afterwards aided in the defense of Tlascala against Cortez. But the surviving warriors carried back to their people such terrible accounts of slaughter and the prowess of the foe, who seemed to be armed with supernatural weapons, that the tribe became panic-stricken and resolved in council upon flight beyond the reach of the as yet invisible invader.

The entire tribe, so legend ran, carrying its movable effects, began an easterly line of march. After a journey of many months it found itself at the headquarters of the Red River. Here it found a suitable place for settlement which it was felt was sufficiently remote from the terrible enemy. It remained in this place for several years and then proceeded northward to the Missouri, and thence to the Mississippi. From there the tribe moved to Ohio. This progress was not by any continuous march but by periodic advances, interrupted by settlements more or less long in duration and marked by conflicts with other local tribes. The Creek were making one of their intermittent advances southward when De Soto came in contact with them in the region of the Coosa.

According to the other tradition, more generally accepted among the Creek, the tribe had originally been a wandering clan from the northwest, beyond the Mississippi. They had made their way down to the present country of the Seminoles. Meeting with plenty of game there, they settled themselves in the vicinity of the then powerful Florida and Appalachian Indians. For some time they remained on friendly footing with one another. These wanderers from the north increased and finally became so powerful as to excite the jealousy of the Appalachians. War ensued and finally the Seminoles, or "wanderers" or "lost men" as they were called, became masters of the country.

In time the game of the country ran thin, and to support

their growing numbers some clans of the Seminoles emigrated northward to Alabama to take possession of the Coweta district. Having established themselves there other emigrations followed, and in time the Alabama Seminoles, now called Creeks, spread themselves eastward as far as the Okmulgee River, and other waters of Georgia and South Carolina westward as far as the Tallapoosa and Coosa rivers, the main branches of the Alabama. There they encountered the Alabama Nation, which they conquered. By restoring the Alabamas' lands to the tribe they gained their friendship, and incorporated them into the Creek Nation.

The Spaniards found no gold in Alabama, and by their brutality and viciousness reaped only the hatred of the Indians along their line of march. Pushing southwestward, De Soto found his way barred by the warriors of the Choctaw. The Spaniards' horrifying firearms won them victories, but the Indian bow and arrow cost them dear in men and horses.

Other gold-crazed Spaniards followed De Soto, but the Indians of Alabama and Georgia were practically untouched by European influence for another century. They received trade goods from the Floridas by intertribal barter, but no more armed men on horseback attacked their stockaded towns.

The next Europeans to enter the southern interior were the French. Like the Spaniards they planned to exploit the Indian, but for a different reason—his furs. To develop the fur trade it was essential to gain control of the river basins. *Coureurs de bois* and fur traders, scouting for beaver, came in touch with the Choctaw, the Chickasaw and the Creek. From the town of Mobile, French trade goods began to make their appearance into the country of the Creek tribes. But these goods were inferior to those of the English traders, who had already crossed the mountains of Virginia and the Carolinas and discovered the Tennessee Valley and the rich fur regions beyond. The great fur war between the French and the British began.

In 1714 the French, hoping to check penetration of the British traders, built Fort Toulouse, near Little Tallassie. Twenty-two years later they erected Fort Tombigbee on the Tombigbee River to dominate the Choctaw and the Chickasaw. The French were successful with the Choctaw, who became their allies, but the Chickasaw, who boasted that they had never lifted the war ax against the English, were won over by English traders.

The British emerged victorious in their struggle for the continent and the long fur war ended. Indian trade was systematized by the British. Prices were fixed, traders licensed and all matters affecting the Indians placed under the control of a superintendent of Indian affairs. Scotch and English traders, among them Lachlan McGillivray, pushed into the region. Many of them married Indian women, lived in the Indian towns and rose to positions of authority in tribal life. Scotch names became commonplace throughout the Creek Confederacy.

Along with territory in the vicinity of Mobile, the British bought from the Indians a huge strip of land reaching far up the Tombigbee River. Settlers began pouring into the Alabama territory from Georgia and the Carolinas, and the Indian began to wonder if white settlement did not bode evil for his possession of his hunting grounds.

Doubt turned to angry certainty when white settlers encroached upon Indian lands. Incidents, bloodshed and conflict inevitably followed. This situation was complicated by the fact that in the course of their trading with the merchants of Georgia the Indians had fallen heavily into debt. In order to settle the claims of their white creditors the Governor of Georgia called a conference at Augusta in 1733. It had a disastrous outcome for the red man; he was forced to cede an

immense area of over two million acres extending as far
north as the Broad River.

Thus there could be no doubt that the Indian was the
natural foe of the American people and therefore the natural
ally of the British in the current conflict between the colonies
and Britain. But to what extent should the Indian ally himself with the British in this war? Wholly, risking all his
strength and substance, or only partly, against the possibility,
however unlikely, that the Americans would win the war
and then take double vengeance on their red-skinned enemy?

To answer this question one had to correctly assess southern
Indian strength. The southern Indians were divided into five
lax confederacies—the Cherokee, Chickasaw, Choctaw, Creek
and Seminole, an offshoot of the Creek. The southern tribes
were probably far more numerous than the northern and
northwestern Indians, the Algonquin tribes. In all they
amounted probably to seventy thousand; it was difficult to
tell the population of the different southern tribes because
the dividing lines between them were ill-defined and subject
to wide fluctuations; ambitious chiefs were constantly forming new settlements.

The Cherokee, some twelve thousand strong, were the
mountaineers of their race, living among the ridges and peaks
of the southern Alleghenies. To the east of the Cherokee, on
the banks of the Mississippi, were the Chickasaw, smallest of
the southern nations. Probably the Chickasaw numbered less
than five thousand, yet theirs was the tribal confederacy that
was most closely knit. Consequently, although engaged in incessant warfare with the far more numerous Choctaw, Creek
and Cherokee, they had more than held their own against
them all; moreover, the Chickasaw had inflicted on the
French the bloodiest defeats they had ever suffered at the
hands of the Indians.

The Choctaw, who lived south of the Chickasaw, and were
smaller in population than the Creek, were primitive and

treacherous, yet shrewd enough to avoid making war as a unit. Most often they acted as auxiliaries of one of the rival European powers, or joined in the war parties of other Indian tribes who attacked the white settlements.

The Creek, between twenty-five thousand and thirty thousand, were the strongest of all. The Upper Creek dwelt along the Coosa and Tallapoosa rivers; the Lower Creek lived further east, on the Chattahoochee and Flint rivers. However, three-fourths of them were Seminoles, living in Florida, south of the Cherokee and east of the Choctaw, adjoining the Georgians. Creek territory was large, probably over ninety thousand square miles.

Thus the Creek and the Cherokee, by geography, were the barrier tribes of the South who must stand the brunt of the settlers' advance and who also acted as a buffer between the Americans and the Spaniards of the Gulf and the lower Mississippi.

Any informed and candid American would have to admit that as a fighting man the Indian was superior to the white. Although the frontiersman was more numerous and a better shot with a rifle, he could not approach the red man in surprise attack nor in the skill of taking advantage of cover. And in military discipline he was much inferior; a settlement captain could not command his men, who obeyed him just so far as it suited them individually. If a white officer planned a scouting trip or a campaign, those who wished to accompany him did so, and the others stayed at home.

Yet the unity of the southern Indians was even more seriously lacking than that of the whites. The southern tribes had fought too many wars and claimed too much disputed territory among themselves to consider banding together against the white settlers, nor did they have chiefs with vision enough to recognize this new threat of a unified thirteen colonies. So far as the Creek Confederacy was itself concerned, as an effective governmental unit it fell far short of the Six Nations of the Iroquois League and still further short of the Aztec and Inca empires.

The so-called Creek Confederacy had never really functioned. There was no central authority, and each town acted as it pleased, making war or peace with other towns, or with whites or other neighboring tribes. In each town there was a head for peace and a head for war—the high chief and the head warrior. The former, though elected for life from one of the powerful clans, had little actual control and could do little more than influence or advise their people. They were dependent on the will of the majority.

Each town was a hotbed of factionalism, with the inhabitants divided on almost every question. The head chief might be for peace, but if the war chief was for taking the warpath there was no way of restraining him. It was said that never in the memory of the oldest Creek had half the nation "taken the war talk" at the same time. Consequently Creek war parties generally were merely small bands of undisciplined marauders in search of scalps and plunder.

A more accurate way of looking at the Creek Nation was to think of it as consisting of several score of tribes called towns which were regarded as the largest natural units.

No, thought Alex, if the survival of the Indians in the American-English war depended upon their joining forces in an effective way, they would go under. And for this reason the southern Indian should choose neutrality over engagement in the white man's war, for he was not strong enough to tip the balance in Britain's favor or to withstand a concerted American attack.

Although many elders of the tribe had reached the same conclusion, the majority of the young warriors were in favor of committing the Nation's strength against the Americans in hopes of crushing them before they grew stronger. Charles Weatherford was among the leaders of this group.

The year before, when Weatherford had been reprimanded in Council for public drunkenness, he had further displeased the elders by accepting their strictures with an air of patronizing arrogance. But from the deference accorded him by other young braves it was apparent that he held a position of influence among them, and gossip was that in time he would become the chief warrior of the town.

In December, on his twentieth birthday, Alex automatically took his seat in Council as a member of the Wind Clan. He was given the name *Hoboi-Hili-Mico,* or the Good Child King. His first vote was cast that day, in opposition to a military expedition against a border settlement of Georgians accused of murdering a Creek scout. When the meeting was over Weatherford came up to him outside. The warrior, clad in breechclout and cape, eyed Alex's shirt and breeches disapprovingly. He said, "I had hoped you would stand with the younger men."

"It wasn't proved that the Georgians were guilty. In fact, all the evidence points to outlaws, or persons unknown."

"I disagree," said Weatherford definitely. "In any case, how will we younger men of Little Tallassie ever take our rightful place in Council unless we stand together against the old men?"

"When I feel you are right I will cast my ballot with you," Alex answered.

His cousin's lip curled. "The day of the peace men among the Creek is ending. Perhaps you've lived too long among the white man to understand that. Or is it that you're so afraid of war that it addles your judgment?"

"Your assumption is false," said Alex coolly. "And one thing is certain—insults will not affect my judgment." He walked away.

At home he found his mother and sisters all agog. For some weeks now Benjamin Durant, a young South Carolinian of Huguenot blood, had been courting Sophia. He was an impressive youth, handsome, strong and intelligent, a match in every way for the vibrant, forthright and beautiful Sophia. That morning he had challenged to a fight a Tallassie brave named Blue Bear who was champion of the Nation. The contest would be held at the Hickory Ground in the afternoon.

Alex wondered aloud why Sophia did not find the news alarming. If Durant should lose the contest, by Creek tradition he could no longer remain in the Nation.

"That's true," agreed Sophia, "but if Benjamin wins he can ask Father for my hand, and be sure of getting it. Along with one of his estates."

Alex shook his head in rueful admiration. "My sister, you have the gambling spirit."

Sophia laughed. "Oh, not all that much. If Benjamin loses I've agreed to run away with him to Charles Town."

A short time later Alex received a message from Benjamin Durant asking him to be his second in the contest. Alex, who liked the French youth, agreed.

News of the challenge had swept the town and there was a large crowd gathered at the Hickory Ground, a large park-like area near the huge oak tree that had overlooked such contests from the earliest days of Creek settlement along the Coosa.

Many warriors were there—Charles Weatherford among them—with their shaved and crested heads, and their lank black hair ornamented with pendent silver quills and jointed silver plates. Most of them wore a diadem or band encircling their temples, decorated with stones, beads and wampum. They also wore ruffled shirts of fine linen and a kiltlike flap of blue cloth that covered their lower parts. For this important occasion—the possible crowning of a new champion, one of the white race—almost all the warriors wore their best mantles of fine scarlet or blue, fancifully decorated with rich lace around the border and silver bells. Their arms were ornamented with silver bands or bracelets, and suspended by a ribbon around their necks hung large silver crescents or gorgets. Their feet were shod in cloth boots reaching from ankle to calf and decorated with lace, beads and silver bells. It was good weather for December and the warrior's shirts were open at the neck. One could see part of their upper chests tattooed with hieroglyphics, scrolls, flowers and figures of animals. The braves joked and talked among themselves, making wagers and eyeing the young women. They stood apart from the older men of the town, the elders and venerable chiefs, who sat in a dignified group, smoking their pipes and waiting for the fight to begin.

The women stood or sat apart in still another grouping. They wore flaps or petticoats larger and longer than those of the men, reaching almost to the middle of the leg. Also a short waistcoat of printed linen calico, or fine cloth, decorated with lace or beads. Their footwear were buskins, reaching almost to the knee.

Their hair was plaited in wreaths which were turned up and fastened on the crown with a silver brooch, forming a wreathed topknot, decorated with an incredible quantity of silk ribbons of various colors, which streamed down on every side almost to the ground. There was no paint on their faces.

Like the men the young women were dressed in their best clothes; usually they wore only a jacket, flap and buskins or moccasins, except in the colder weather when, as the men, they went about with a mantle thrown over their shoulders.

In still another group stood the junior priests, dressed in their white mantles. These were their mark of distinction, along with the stuffed owls with sparkling eyes of glass beads which they carried on their arms. Typically, they wore a grave and solemn expression on their taciturn faces.

The last two groups consisted of the younger boys and girls from eleven to fifteen years of age. They were segregated as to sex and both were dressed in flap jackets, moccasins or buskins. On their fringes a few male youths, naked except for flaps, frisked and fooled.

Benjamin Durant arrived on time although Blue Bear, his opponent, had not yet appeared. Alex showed him the bucket of water and plentiful supply of towels he had brought with him, and the Frenchman nodded approvingly.

"What are your instructions?" asked Alex.

Durant laughed, white teeth showing in his tanned face—the Huguenot's complexion was darker than Sophia's, who was absent for traditional reasons. "Instructions? If Blue Bear kills me, bury me beneath your sister's window. If I beat him, do your best to prevent his fellow braves from hanging me to this oak."

There was an admiring murmur as Blue Bear, accompanied by his second, stepped through the crowd. Alex had seen the Creek champion before, but never stripped to his flap, and he seemed terrifying. He was huge, at least six feet four, with knots of muscle that bunched and rippled as he squatted at his edge of the clearing. His wooden face was impassive, betraying not a flicker of emotion. He made a fine champion, a man who had defeated not only every challenger in the Creek Confederacy for the past four years, but challengers from the Cherokee and Choctaw. The Creek warriors idolized him, not least because he had won so many wagers for them.

What chance had Benjamin to defeat this man, Alex wondered. True, the Frenchman was a superb athlete, and he had amazing strength. On the ball field he had seen him perform prodigious feats of skill and coordination. But he was at least five inches shorter than his opponent, and in weight, girth and reach, considerably inferior.

Durant saw what Alex was thinking. "Don't worry, future brother-in-law," he said. "I shall be the David to defeat this Goliath. I have studied him and know the way to bring him down."

Opilth Mico, high chief of Little Tallassie, was acting as referee. He called the contestants and their seconds forward for instructions. Unlike fights of backwoodsmen style, in which no holds were barred, the Indian contests of strength had definite rules. Disallowed were eye-gouging, groin-kneeing and the breaking of bones. If the referee ruled that a contestant was guilty of any of these infractions his opponent was instantly declared the winner. The fight continued until one contestant had pinioned his antagonist to the ground in two of three falls, or rendered him senseless and unable to continue. Only after a contestant had registered a fall was he allowed to be refreshed by his second.

The contestants returned to their corners, the chief raised his hand in signal and the bout began.

Durant's strategy was immediately clear. He was to be the hornet to the bear, stinging him to madness, then zooming away, only to return again to the attack from a different quarter. Alex gasped at the agility Durant displayed in eluding the Indian's first ponderous rushes and lunges. He danced, he sidestepped, he flicked in and away like a sword blade, usually managing to land a blow. Already the Creek had a bruise under his eye.

And yet Durant's method had its dangers, too. Once he tired or slowed down, the Creek would catch and crush him in his grip like a bear would a hickory nut. Inevitably one of the Indian's blows caught the Frenchman on the side of the head and the crowd grunted as he slipped to one knee, shaking his head groggily. But Blue Bear was a second too late in following up his opportunity. The knee he directed at his antagonist's chin missed its mark as the Frenchman rolled away, and the Creek went sprawling.

With incredible speed Durant was on his back, grasping for an arm and twisting it, using it as a lever to keep Blue Bear to the ground. The Indian, for all his strength, was helpless; if he moved Durant would break his arm.

Opilth Mico counted out fifteen seconds, then raised his arm, signifying the first fall in favor of the Frenchman. The spectators groaned. Charles Weatherford's face showed his disappointment.

Alex had expected Benjamin to come to his corner for a drink and toweling, but the Frenchman though bathed in perspiration, did not call time out but immediately attacked his opponent as soon as he had risen, swinging blows at his head, pounding his body, ducking his roundhouse swings, any one of which would have sent him reeling had it connected. By now both men were dripping with sweat, which turned out to be an advantage to Durant, for the Frenchman slipped and the Creek champion succeeded in grappling with him, but in a moment he had twisted out of Blue Bear's grasp.

The pattern continued as before, Indian stalking white man, white man eluding him to land a stinging blow and then dance maddeningly away. Alex looked for signs of fatigue in the Frenchman, but he seemed inexhaustible. On the other hand, Blue Bear's breathing was already labored and his movements less decisive.

At this moment the Creek did not look like the champion that he was. Perhaps that was one of the secrets of his success, for in the next instant the tables were turned abruptly. One of his swings caught Durant on the temple and the Frenchman went down to his knees. As the crowd roared the Creek leapt upon him, pinning Durant to the ground. Opilth Mico called a fall for the Indian.

This time Blue Bear elected to call time out. Alex sluiced Benjamin's head and chest with water and toweled him off. Durant grinned at his anxiety. "Do not count me out," he said. "I will still be Sophia's David."

Alex would have felt better about his chances had Durant produced, then and there, the equivalent of a slingshot, or some other secret weapon.

The chief raised his arm to renew the contest. Durant got slowly to his feet. His first steps into the clearing were halting, tentative. Blue Bear, visibly expanding with confidence, a smile touching his wooden lips, moved forward, rising from his cautious crouch. Then the Frenchman—there was no other word for it—exploded into action. He lunged in a tackle so blinding in its speed that few in the crowd could follow it.

In moments the fight was over. Durant, astride the recumbent Indian, lifted his head by its crest of hair and slammed it to the ground. He slammed it to the earth again, and as he did so Alex saw the rock against which the Creek's head was being banged. Durant had downed the Indian in such a way that when he lay full length the rock lay ready to hand as a weapon.

Blue Bear's body relaxed, his hands unclenched. He was unconscious.

Durant got to his feet, chest heaving. Opilth Mico raised an arm in token of his victory.

For a moment there was complete silence. Then a great shout went up, and the Creek warriors rushed forward to congratulate the Frenchman and carry him on their shoulders to Little Tallassie in triumph. It was forgotten that Blue Bear had been their favorite; they were a generous people and had already taken the white man, their new champion, to their hearts.

Benjamin Durant had won his gamble. And Sophia, hers.

A week later, after Lachlan McGillivray's return home from a trip to Augusta, Benjamin and Sophia were married.

They were married as Sophia's father and mother had been, and with the same simple but binding ceremonies.

In the Creek Confederacy a young man intent on marriage first obtained the consent of the girl's parents. Then, taking a cane or a reed, and attended by his friends, he went to her lodge and in the presence of the wedding guests struck his reed upright into the ground. His fiancée then struck another reed by the side of his.

The reeds were exchanged, then laid aside as certificates of marriage. Feasting, music and dancing followed for two days, during which relatives and friends contributed presents. Colonel Tait, taking his disappointment manfully, presented the couple with a silver service.

In usual cases the Town Council recommended a new lodge to be built for the new couple. Every able-bodied man in the town was expected to join in the work, which was finished in a day's time. But Benjamin and Sophia's case was not a usual one, since Sophia was the daughter of a very wealthy man. As a wedding gift Lachlan McGillivray gave the couple an estate a few miles from his own plantation, and construction was begun immediately on a plantation house with a view of the Coosa River. Until the house was complete—since it was wartime this would take at least two years—Benjamin and Sophia would live at the Little Tallassie plantation house. Benjamin, whose funds had just about run out, took over the duties of assistant overseer of his father-in-law's plantations.

In later years the McGillivrays were to laugh at what then occurred in the family's marital fortunes—the appearance on the scene of still another Frenchman, who fell in love with the sixteen-year-old Jeannet and promptly sued for her hand.

Louis Milfort was a young man, twenty-five years old, who had arrived in New York, joined a New York regiment at the beginning of the hostilities with Britain, "left" before his period of service expired, and gone to Charles Town. Hearing of the beauty of the Creek country, and that white men were welcome there, he had visited its major towns and finally arrived in Little Tallassie, where he introduced himself to Lachlan McGillivray. The hospitable Scot invited him to be his guest at the plantation while Milfort "compiled information on the Creek Nation for a book."

Milfort had a refreshing candor. The young Frenchman

did not represent himself as anything other than what he was —an adventurer to whom the principles of more ordinary men were a luxury he could ill afford. He did not hide the fact that he had deserted the Continental army because the food was bad and he had no valet. He readily volunteered the information that he had supported himself in Charles Town by fleecing the sons of planters and merchants at cards, and by betting on the cocking mains and horse races.

Never had an adventurer looked less the part. Milfort was slight in build, and weighed no more than a hundred and forty pounds. He had stooped shoulders. His eyes were weak and for close work he wore spectacles. His hairline was receding. He looked like nothing more than an underpaid clerk.

Yet Milfort's appearance was only another weapon in his arsenal to confuse his opponents and lead them astray. Although slight he had great stamina and endurance, as the wiry often do. Though nearsighted, he had a dazzling proficiency with the rapier, and with a pistol could hit a leaf at forty yards. He could drink half a bottle of taffia, the strong local rum, with no evident effect. And at the card table he was a master.

Lachlan McGillivray lost ten pounds to him at whist, which the Frenchman then tactfully lost back, to the penny. The entire family was witness to Milfort's encyclopedic familiarity with Shakespeare, whom he not only quoted but acted out. His Hamlet was as convincing as his Falstaff. It was like going to the theater in your parlor.

Yet this did not end the catalogue of Milfort's skills. He knew hairdressing, and delighted Sehoy and her daughters with his imaginative creations. He was an expert dancer and could teach the most intricate steps. He knew dressmaking, upholstering, winemaking, architecture and interior design— not to mention history, engineering and military science.

Such was Milfort's curious charm that he had won Jeannet's heart within a week of his stay at the plantation. The

Frenchman declared his love, and his paeans to her attractions of mind, soul and body were endless.

Lachlan McGillivray was far from pleased with this development. As a guest Louis Milfort was pleasant, indeed delightful. He would hate to see him go. But as a husband for his youngest daughter—why the man was, by his own admission, a deserter, a cardsharp, an adventurer. Nothing solid to him. Marriage was out of the question.

But Jeannet was a young girl in love and stubborn. "Why is he so different from Benjamin?" she demanded. "He is French and poor, he appeared suddenly in Little Tallassie, he asked for my hand."

"Benjamin's a strong man, a hard worker, a person of character," her father grumbled. "Milfort is nothing more than an accomplished fop. How can you be sure he loves you?"

"Must he pass a test, like Benjamin?" asked Jeannet.

"I have no tests for him to pass," Lachlan McGillivray said sourly, "and neither do the Creeks, who look at him askance already, and with good reason. No, young lady, you had best forget him, for his stay here will be over at the end of the week."

Milfort came to Alexander for help. There was only one course open to him, he said—he and Jeannet must run away. They would be married in Charles Town, and would perhaps return to Little Tallassie later. Meanwhile he needed a loan, which would be returned at his earliest opportunity. Could Alex oblige him?

Alex told the Frenchman regretfully that he had no ready money and that in any case he could not go against his father's wishes in the matter. He would do nothing to hinder Milfort, but neither could he help.

"*Eh bien,* I understand," said Milfort, shrugging his stooped shoulders. The next day he left Little Tallassie.

Jeannet was inconsolable. Lachlan McGillivray became so

unnerved by her hysterical carryings-on that he set off for Savannah on a business trip that had been scheduled for later in the year. Alex, as the man of the house, was left to bear the brunt of Jeannet's weeping and wailing. Had not Sehoy prepared an herbal brew that somewhat calmed his sister, he would have been at his wit's end.

When Lachlan returned Jeannet was worse; for days now she had refused to eat and had lapsed into a melancholia which had the family fearing for her sanity. Sehoy's herbal remedies did no real good; the only thing that could cure her was Louis Milfort.

Lachlan gave in, and Benjamin Durant was sent to Charles Town to fetch Milfort. The Frenchman returned to Little Tallassie with a new wardrobe and presents for all the family; the cards had been kind to him during his weeks of exile.

The wedding was held in February, 1777. Lachlan McGillivray's gift was a house and estate downriver near Benjamin and Sophia's. Milfort went to work in his father-in-law's trading enterprises. To the surprise of everyone except Jeannet he pitched in with a will and did fairly well, although it was obvious that his natural talents did not include those of moneymaking by conventional or respectable means.

VI

WAR IN THE SOUTH

The British renewed their attack on the South in the winter of 1778–1779. Savannah and its small force under General Benjamin Lincoln fell to British Lieutenant Colonel Archibald Campbell on December 29.

Meanwhile British General Sir George Prevost was marching north through Georgia from Florida. He captured several posts without difficulty and, passing on to Savannah, effected junction with Campbell, took command of the united force and dispatched Campbell upriver to attack Augusta. Augusta was also taken without serious opposition. Campbell proceeded to establish various armed posts in western Georgia.

By the end of 1779 the British conquest of Georgia was complete. In May of the following year they captured Charles Town, quickly reduced all South Carolina to submission and then marched into the older northern state.

General Cornwallis was in command of a mixed force of British, Hessian and Loyalist American regulars, aided by Irish volunteers and bodies of refugees from Florida. In addition, Loyalists, very numerous in the southern states, rose at once at the news of the British successes, and a number of regiments of Tory militia were formed.

British agents among the Cherokee were successful in enlisting warriors for the King's standard, and this, in addition to the undeniable British successes, encouraged British agents among the Creek to attempt the same.

This time the more cautious chiefs could not stand up to

General Charles Cornwallis, as painted by Copley

the warriors, who demanded immediate collaboration with the British and Tories to extinguish the American threat. In Grand Council the vote was heavily in favor of sending Creek bands to assist the British and Tories on the frontier. Only Alexander McGillivray and a few others were against such collaboration.

On the evening that Alexander returned home from Coweta, where the Grand Council had been held, Colonel Tait dropped in at the plantation house to see him. He was direct and to the point. The British were interested in seeing to it that the Creeks collaborated more fully with the British and Tory forces. By virtue of his birth and abilities Alex would bear increasing weight in tribal councils. It was to the British interest to keep him happy. Would he accept a royal commission as captain and the emoluments and uniforms that went with the rank?

Alex smiled. "I admire your candor, John, but I'm not bribable. You know how I stand on this issue."

"Why not go with the tide? Maintain your stand and you'll be suspected of sympathizing secretly with the Americans. This can only do you harm, and I know you are ambitious."

"I do not deny my ambition. But the interests of my people are first in my heart. You, of course, serve your own people, and may I remind you that before the war it was to British advantage to keep the Indian nations fighting among themselves, so that they would leave the Anglo-American settlers in peace?"

Tait reddened. "The situation has changed. You cannot deny that it would be good for the Creek should the Americans be defeated. Why not join with us, and the Loyalist militia, in that task?"

"Because I am none too sure you will succeed. And should you fail, with the Creek Nation as your fully committed ally, the vengeance of the Americans will be terrible. We must avoid that vengeance at all costs, for even if their revolution is crushed they will still be on our borders after the peace treaty has been signed."

Tait sighed. "There is an old expression, Alex: 'The wise man strikes while the iron is hot.'"

"I would differ with you, however, on the hotness of this particular iron. Also on our enemy's possession of some irons that are very hot indeed."

Tait cleared his throat and said, "I must tell you something unpleasant, Alex. My instructions are to confer a captaincy upon your outstanding younger leader. Since you refuse it, I have no choice but to offer the commission to Charles Weatherford."

"He'll be overjoyed to wear a smart British shortcoat with his flap," Alex said, more calmly than he felt. That he should have handed this triumph to Weatherford personally! Especially when, before the month's end, he was to be married to Janine Magnaque, the attractive daughter of a half-breed trader. He should take a captaincy for Janine's sake as much as his own. For a moment Alex was tempted to tell Tait he had changed his mind.

The colonel broke the silence. "By the way, would you like to meet Patrick Ferguson? He'll be in Little Tallassie next week."

"Ferguson in Little Tallassie?"

"Yes, on a trip raising Loyalists to the King's standard, with his second-in-command, Lieutenant Colonel de Peyster. I have invited him to meet the Creek chiefs, and will be his host here."

"I would be delighted," Alex said. Ferguson was the current hero of the Loyalist South, and his name had been on everybody's lips for weeks now.

Patrick Ferguson, the son of a lord, was a Scotch soldier about thirty-six years old. For twenty years he had served with distinction in the British army, and became known as its best marksman with pistol and rifle. Two years ago he had been given command of a company of riflemen in the army facing Washington around New York. At Brandywine he suffered a wound that had made his right arm useless; yet he had trained himself to shoot almost as well with his left. At Monmouth none other than George Washington had been in his sights, but out of gallantry he had forborne to pull the trigger.

When the British occupied New York Ferguson was given command of several small independent expeditions, all of which he managed successfully. On one, in particular, he surprised and routed Pulaski's legion, creating great havoc with the bayonet, a favorite weapon. Within a month he was famous, and when the British army was sent to reopen the southern campaign he went along as lieutenant colonel of a recently raised regiment of Tories known as the American Volunteers.

Cornwallis, ablest of the British generals, recognized Ferguson's fitness for the special kind of warfare the British would be waging in the South—sudden attacks, surprises and swift movements by both day and night. Not only was Ferguson an able leader, but he had a quiet personal charm that won people's confidence everywhere. Kind and civil, he had won over countless Patriots to the English side by talking over their problems with them and verbally disposing of their reasons for rebelling against their lawful King. He also had a quick and inventive intelligence, having developed a breech-loading rifle that he had already used to deadly effect in the field.

After the capitulation of Charles Town, Ferguson's volunteers and Colonel Banastre Tarleton's legion, acting separately and often together, quickly destroyed the last vestiges of Patriot resistance. Their success was such that American commanders lost all hope of coping with them, as one after another Patriot detachment was routed.

But while the people of the South came to hate and loathe Banastre Tarleton for his brutal ruthlessness, mistreatment of civilians and outright massacres, Ferguson was respected for his mercy and generosity; it was well known that he severely punished those of his partisan troopers who outraged Patriot women.

Lieutenant Colonel Patrick Ferguson of the American Volunteers was of middle height and slender build. His shy smile was singularly winning, and Alex liked him on sight. Talking with the partisan leader, dressed in his uniform of bright green, Alex discovered that intellectually he was a

Lt. Col. Banastre Tarleton, as painted by Sir Joshua Reynolds

strange combination of orthodoxy and original thinking. On
the one hand, the ideas Ferguson put forward against the
Revolution were no different from what Alex had heard a
hundred times before from Loyalists who parroted the Tory
pamphleteers: Congress was an illegal body; law, under
King and Parliament, was preferable to "liberty" under

armed mobs; the colonial assemblies might be left to raise
general revenue, but Parliament should provide for the
general defense of the colonies by levying duties on American trade.

Yet, although he was raising the back country to enlist
Loyalist troops, Ferguson was perfectly frank about what he
felt was the future of the Tory cause, and its weaknesses.

"Yes, Mr. McGillivray," he said, "I quite agree with your
way of thinking. The Tories are weak, and their basic weakness is not their attachment to Britain; that is a *consequence*
of their weakness; rather, their weakness lies in the fact that
they hold social and political opinions which can prevail in
America only with British assistance."

Ferguson had put it well, thought Alex. He said: "The
Tories are afraid to submit these opinions to the American
public for its approval or rejection. The result is that the
weaker the Tories feel themselves to be, the tighter becomes
their allegiance to Britain, and the closer they are bound to
Britain the less able will they be to support effectively her
cause or theirs. And this attachment, growing desperate, will
cease to be honorable in the end."

Ferguson smiled. "Reasoned, sir, like William Pitt." But
his aide, Colonel de Peyster, was less enthusiastic. Tossing
off the last of his brandy in an irritable way, he returned the
glass to the table with a force that almost broke it. "Damn
it all, McGillivray," he said, "I don't know how you can talk
that way when Tory troops are making the South safe for
you."

"That's precisely what I deny," Alex answered. "Tory
troops are regarded by the frontiersmen as criminals rather
than ordinary foes. The struggle in the Carolinas and
Georgia will take—has begun to take on already—the form of
a ferocious civil war. Now the Tories are in the saddle—they
are murdering, robbing and driving off the Whigs. But in
turn, when the pendulum swings the other way, they will

bring down ferocious reprisals on their own heads, and on those of their allies, the Indians."

"We have almost won the South, and when we do we will keep it," De Peyster boasted. "There's no need for you southern Indians to be concerned."

"Sorry, Colonel," Alex told him with a grin, "but we Creeks are worriers."

Ferguson's mission to the Creek towns was not notably successful, mostly because those warriors, including Charles Weatherford, who were inclined to fight on the frontier had already left on expeditions. However, Louis Milfort, who had been won over by Ferguson's charm, announced that he was departing at the head of a small band of warriors for the Georgia border. Jeannet had objections and Lachlan McGillivray gave his permission reluctantly, on condition that his new son-in-law return within a month or two.

Congress had chosen the three commanders under whom Savannah and Charles Town, Georgia and the Carolinas had been lost to the British. Now it called upon Washington to select a new commander for the southern army. He chose Nathanael Greene, whose armies were to consist of all the Continental regiments raised or to be raised from Delaware to Georgia.

Greene arrived in Charlotte, North Carolina and soon gained the support of the famous partisan leaders Morgan, Marion, Sumter and Pickens. His effective strength was only a little over 2,000 men, but he succeeded within three months in increasing this to over 4,400. This was the force that, aided by the guerrillas Sumter, Pickens and others, and varying from nothing to perhaps a maximum of 2,000, set out to reconquer the South. The British had perhaps 11,000 men fit for duty, exclusive of officers. About three-fourths of these were regulars, British and Hessian, and the rest were seasoned Tory regiments from New York and New Jersey.

Cornwallis meanwhile had not been idle. He had marched

unopposed into North Carolina as far as Charlotte; and Clinton had sent 3,000 men to the Chesapeake to act there under Cornwallis' orders and effect a junction with him as he marched north. These plans miscarried; for, soon after Cornwallis had reached Charlotte and before Clinton's detachment had sailed from New York, a force of backwoodsmen, about 1,500 strong, who lived in the mountains from Virginia to Georgia, suddenly appeared as if they had sprung from the ground. At King's Mountain they surrounded Ferguson's regular and Tory militia of about 1,100 men.

Ferguson had been posted in the foothills of the Alleghenies, on Cornwallis' left flank, about thirty miles from Charlotte. He took a defensive position on the top of King's Mountain, a wooded hill just north of the boundary between North and South Carolina. Here, on the autumn afternoon of October 7, the battle was joined.

Dismounting from their horses, the mountaineers swarmed up the hill on all sides, using their rifles with great effect. Ferguson's defense was a gallant one. Three times, using the bayonet, he beat back the mountaineers. After an hour of hard fighting Ferguson was killed and his men surrounded. He had lost 224 killed and 163 wounded; over 700 Tories and regulars were taken prisoner. On the American side only 28 lost their lives, and 60 were wounded.

News of the American victory spread like wildfire. It brought out the militia of North Carolina and new levies in Virginia; it plunged the Tories in both Carolinas into gloom. Stunned by Ferguson's defeat and death at King's Mountain, disappointed in his hopes that North Carolina would rally to his support, Cornwallis not only halted his invasion but hastily retreated to South Carolina.

The Creek bands that had been ravaging the frontier returned home. Louis Milfort straggled back to Little Tallassie with no scalps taken and a trivial amount of booty. And Alexander McGillivray, the only Council member of any conse-

The death of Patrick Ferguson in the Battle of King's Mountain

quence who had voted against taking the warpath against
the Americans, was elected Chief and Spokesman of the
Little Tallassie Creeks. He was twenty-two years old.

Throughout America the people had given unmistakable
evidence that no Loyalist would be tolerated among them.
Even those Tory refugees who, after various British defeats,
had joined the American army, had never been too gra-
ciously received. By 1780 all of the states had plainly defined

the traitor as one who adhered to the King of Great Britain. He who by preaching, teaching, speaking or writing maintained that the King had authority over the states of New Jersey, Delaware or Pennsylvania, or who acknowledged allegiance to Great Britain, should suffer death without benefit of clergy, confiscation of his property or banishment.

The state of Georgia, perhaps because its major cities were constantly threatened by British recapture, was the last to revenge itself on the Loyalists. In 1777 it had passed an act for the expulsion of the internal enemies of the state, and, two years later, an act empowering committees to examine the conduct of suspicious persons. But these acts were enforced only casually. However, in 1780 legislation was passed confiscating the estates of proscribed Loyalists and banishing them forever.

The name of Lachlan McGillivray headed the list of Georgia Loyalists. He was given sixty days to wind up his affairs and leave the country.

The news was a tremendous blow to the aging Scot and his family. Lachlan McGillivray was an American. It was in the Colonies that he had put down new roots, married and raised a family and built his impressive career. Now his life was shattered.

"Was the Spanish Inquisition worse?" he raged. "What is my crime against my neighbors—that I have refused to renounce a solemn oath of allegiance to my King? That I hold unpopular opinions? What other modern civilized country can present such a spectacle of the wholesale disposal of the rights, liberties, property and even lives of its citizens?"

Alex felt the blow almost as keenly. Not only was he losing the father he loved, but his mother was prostrate; she knew that Scotland, to which her husband must return, was no place for a woman of mixed blood; she must lose him, too. And not only that—the McGillivrays, in one stroke, had been reduced from the status of wealthy property owners to that of ordinary farmers. Although the Alabama plantations were unaffected by the edict—thank the Lord Alabama was not yet a state!—Lachlan would realize very little from the enforced sale of his Augusta and Savannah business properties.

"We have one hope," the distraught Scot told his family, "that after the war my properties will be returned. They will be yours then, Alex, for surely by that time I shall be dead."

Aged years by the disaster, Lachlan left for the coast to liquidate his holdings—a bitter task, for waiting for him were his erstwhile business associates of Patriot convictions, hands outstretched greedily for the rich plums that were shortly to fall. Samuel Elbert, it developed, was among them.

By the end of March Lachlan McGillivray had sailed for Scotland. Accompanying him were the Reverend Farquar and his wife, who had decided there was no longer a place for them in America.

When John Tait approached Alex again with the offer of a colonelcy in the British army, he accepted without hesitation. The Georgians had destroyed his father and separated him from his wife and family. They had deprived his son of his inheritance. Finally, he frankly needed the salary that went along with the British commission. Lachlan had left the family no money apart from a sum put aside for Sehoy that Alexander refused to touch. His wife Janine was expecting a child. Upkeep of the plantation and house was expensive. Had Sophia and Jeannet not been married, with their husbands taking care of their financial needs, he would have been in a very bad position indeed.

The British defeat at King's Mountain did not discourage the Cherokee, who in November, 1780 began attacking the white settlements along the frontier. Their war parties slipped through the countryside burning cabins, taking scalps and stealing horses.

The alarmed and angered settlers of the Holston, the

Tennessee valley both north and south of the Virginia line, joined in sending troops. By the first week in December seven hundred mounted riflemen were ready to march under John Sevier, the best Indian fighter on the border, and Colonel Arthur Campbell.

At the New Year all the country of the Overhill, or Otari, Cherokee had been laid waste with a thousand cabins burned and fifty thousand bushels of corn destroyed. In the burnt towns and on the dead warriors were found many letters from British agents and commanders.

Before returning to their homes the American commanders issued an address to the Cherokee headmen, telling the Indians that they had suffered a just punishment for their folly and perfidy in carrying out the wishes of the British agents. They were warned that unless they treated for peace their country would not only be laid waste but conquered for all time.

Some Cherokee chiefs entered into talks with the Americans, but although anxious for peace, they could not restrain the more vindictive of the young braves. Nor could the white commanders keep the frontiersmen from settling within the acknowledged boundaries of Cherokee territory. When the army marched back from burning the Overhill towns, they found that adventurous settlers had followed in its wake and had already made clearings and built cabins.

In desperation the younger warriors forced their elders to call for aid from the Creeks. A Grand Council was called at Coweta in late 1780. Alexander McGillivray attended as the representative of the Coosa towns. In his entourage were Louis Milfort, Benjamin Durant and Charles Weatherford.

The Cherokee speaker was a handsome warrior of great presence and address. He spoke movingly of how the burning of the Otari's houses and grain had left many of them to starve; of how women and children had fallen from the white man's bullets. He spoke of how the white settlers were encroaching on the Cherokee lands, using the uprisings as their excuse. And he concluded oratorically: "This is not only our fight against extinction, it is your fight, too. For after the white man destroys the Cherokee he will destroy the Choctaw, and after the Choctaw the Chickasaw, and after the Chickasaw, the Creek. Alone we cannot stand against him but together we may dam the stream. If we do not it will become in time a torrent—and then all the red men of the South will drown in blood."

Some Creek chiefs nodded in approval as the Otari warrior sat. He had made some converts. Then Alexander, in Indian dress, rose from his place.

He began by reminding the assembly that twice in recent years the Cherokee had risen, only to be severely punished on both occasions. He knew it was impossible to keep the fiercest of the young braves from harassing the settlements and bringing down retaliation upon the more peaceable Indians' heads. But surely the wise chiefs who were gathered here today must know that any concerted campaign against the settlements in league with an already defeated ally must result in disaster for those Creek towns that sent warriors.

Turning to the smoldering Cherokee he said: "I do not blame you for speaking thus. Indeed my heart is heavy for your losses. But as long as you are weak, as long as you strike back not out of strength but desperation, so long will you suffer great losses. And I predict this: that should you rise still again before you are ready, or should your young braves provoke the enemy, the Watcina will penetrate not only your valleys but your hitherto untrodden wilds. They will wind their way through the deep defiles and among the towering peaks of the Smoky Mountains and descend by the precipitous passes. They will burst out of the woods and fall like a thunderbolt on your towns nestling in the high gorges. They will kill your surprised warriors, burn your villages and carry off your women and children.

"No, friend, do not come to the Creek Nation when you are weak and this is what you must fear from the white man. Come when you are fit, and we will fight together, two strong nations that have the dignity of hope."

Some Creek chiefs murmured their approval of young McGillivray's impressive speech. Others thought that such sentiments were unfitting in one who had accepted honors and gifts from the British, the enemy of the Americans. Still others believed that he had achieved his effect unfairly by predicting a dire event which, after all, was yet to occur. But when the vote was taken only a few towns had elected to assist the Cherokee in any new strikes against their foes.

Alex did not have long to wait to see his prediction fulfilled. Early in March John Sevier, at the head of a hundred and fifty picked horsemen, fell upon the Erati—or mountain—Cherokee. The future first governor of Tennessee stormed their main town, burnt two others, destroyed provisions and captured several hundred horses.

Before the startled Erati could gather their attack Sevier had plunged into the wilderness, moving so swiftly that his pursuers lost his trail. It was the most brilliant exploit of the border war.

The Creek chiefs remembered that Alexander McGillivray had said this would come to pass. Here was a man who, educated in the white man's midst, knew him as did no other Creek living. He was spoken of with awe and admiration in Coweta and Oakfuskee, in Tuckabatches and in Big Ufala. Many said that had the Creek Confederacy been united enough to permit the election of one man as its supreme chief, Alexander McGillivray, despite his youth, would have been so chosen.

That summer peace was made between the settlers and the Cherokee at the Great Island of the Holston. Needless to say, the treaty was not to the Cherokees' benefit or liking.

VII

THE TREATY OF PENSACOLA

In 1779 Spain determined to invade West Florida, lightly occupied by the British, and regain the territory that she had surrendered to Great Britain in 1763. She had an additional goal: to obtain that part of Louisiana on the Gulf of Mexico that Britain had acquired from France. A major expedition under the able Don Bernardo Galvez, governor of Louisiana, was prepared against Pensacola. Earlier Spain had acknowledged the independence of the United States in prearrangements designed to enable the Spaniards to attack British posts in West Florida before they could be strengthened materially.

The British had only twelve hundred men in Pensacola; troops were needed too badly for service in the northern colonies. They determined to call on their allies among the Creek and Choctaw for help.

In March, 1780 Galvez took the British post of Fort Charlotte. But not until February of the next year, the year of Morgan's brilliant victory over the British at Cowpens and Greene's defeat at Guildford Court House, did he move against Pensacola. The British received word that Galvez was about to advance against Pensacola with a large fleet and an army of fifteen thousand men. British agents among the Creek, Choctaw and Chickasaw were ordered to obtain aid from them to help the thin garrison at Pensacola to withstand Galvez' attack.

The British had treated the Indians well and the Spaniards had failed to shake their loyalty; several hundred Choctaw and Chickasaw were recruited as British auxiliaries. Colonel Tait visited the Creek towns and obtained the services of several warrior bands. Alexander McGillivray knew he would be approached by Tait and that the bill for British favors was falling due. But he was unprepared for what Tait told him.

William Augustus Bowles, an American adventurer in his early twenties, had assumed command of the Creek bands and had so impressed the Choctaws and Chickasaws that it was likely he would be given leadership of the entire Indian force. Bowles had a striking personality, great energy and unusual charm; there seemed no limit to his influence over the chiefs of the Lower Creek.

All Alex knew about Bowles was that he had recently settled among the Lower Creeks and married the daughter of a chief. This in itself was far from unusual; many white men had done so and become influential in the councils of their adopted people. Nor was it out of the way that Bowles's background was unsavory; originally an officer in the Maryland Loyalist Corps, he had been cashiered soon after the arrival of his regiment at Pensacola in 1778. The vast majority of white men who came to live among the Indians were fleeing something in their pasts.

What was special about Bowles was the ease with which he had been able to impress not only the Creek chiefs but their neighbors. The Choctaw and the Chickasaw already called him "General."

Colonel Tait knew that the news he brought Alex of a new and active competitor in the Creek Nation would be disturbing to him. He was also hoping, by means of Bowles, to rouse him to more definite efforts in the British behalf than he had so far made.

"Perhaps you will lead Creek contingents to Pensacola yourself?" asked Tait.

"Come, John, we need play no games," Alex told him. "I'm not afraid of this extraordinary fellow. I will send

Milfort and Weatherford with as many warriors as volunteer from the Coosa area. Beyond that I cannot go, not least for the reason that Pensacola is doomed."

Tait nodded; he couldn't pretend that the British had much chance of holding Pensacola against the vastly superior Spanish forces.

Milfort and Weatherford departed for West Florida with three hundred braves, arriving shortly before Galvez attacked in late April. He was beaten back and the Spaniards sustained heavy losses. But Pensacola's Fort George could not sustain the Spaniards' incessant cannonading, and on May 8, the day Alexander McGillivray, Jr. came into the world at Little Tallassie, the British commander hoisted the white flag of surrender. He had firm demands: his troops must be allowed to march out with colors flying and drums beating, and must be shipped at Spanish expense to a British port.

Galvez agreed to these conditions. The next day eight hundred British and their Indian allies marched out from Fort George before the Spanish army. The British stacked their arms; the Indians began their long trip homeward. A short time later the British sailed for Havana, and from there to New York.

The British had lost West Florida, and the defeat was an omen of what was to befall them four months later, when Cornwallis surrendered to Washington at Yorktown, practically ending the Revolutionary War.

Charles Weatherford did not take William Augustus Bowles very seriously. "He is a handsome, likable rogue, and the cutthroats who are his personal bodyguard are completely devoted to him. But he runs from a real fight. When we beat back the Spaniards' first attack at the shoreline, Bowles was safely in the fort, waving us on with his sword."

But Louis Milfort had a different opinion. Bowles, he said, was a fraud, but a dangerous one. Bowles had spent much time questioning various Upper Creek warriors about Alexander, and had managed to convince several that Alexander McGillivray could never lead his Nation because he refused to risk his neck in battle. The turncoat American had definite ambitions to dominate the Creeks as a kind of Great White Father, but his real goal, Milfort said, was not glory, but gold. He wanted to corner the Creek trade.

Now that the war was ending and the Atlantic traders were once more taking the trails that led to western Georgia and eastern Alabama, Alexander had discussed with his brothers-in-law the possibility of dominating, from Little Tallassie, the Creek trade that had languished during the hostilities. Bowles was potentially a threat to this effort, so Alexander was not surprised when Milfort said, "Would it not be a good idea to stop Bowles before he goes much further?"

"You mean murder him?"

"Dead men do not become great traders," Milfort said. Alexander knew he was in perfect earnest. Only a short time ago Milfort had demonstrated that the ability to kill, and with a certain style, was another facet of his complex character.

Colonel Kirkland, a South Carolina Loyalist, and his party had visited Little Tallassie on their way to Mobile, where they planned to settle. Alex had sent his Negro servant Paro to guide them. The Negro's presence would assure the Indians that they were friends; it was dangerous to travel in Creek country without the protection of a well-known chief. Besides, Kirkland's saddlebags were heavy with silver.

The colonel and his party, composed of his son, nephew, several Negroes and other gentlemen, arrived within a mile of a large creek. About sunup they met a pack-horse party on its way to Little Tallassie. This party consisted of a Creek called "The Man-Slayer," who had murdered many white men, a desperado called the "Cat," wanted for murder in the states, and a bloodthirsty Negro named Bob, the property of Sullivan, a white trader of the Hillabee Creek.

Kirkland's party continued on, crossed the creek and encamped a short distance from the ford by the trading path. They had no idea that the pack-horse party had camped a short distance away. At midnight the scoundrels attacked, and killed all the party except three Negroes, one of whom was Paro. Dividing the booty, the murderers proceeded to Little Tallassie. Not knowing that Kirkland and his party had been under Alex's protection, they spoke freely of the crime before moving on.

Alex sent Milfort in pursuit. The Cat was arrested by him, but the others escaped. Alex directed the Frenchman to bring the murderer to the spot of the slaying and hang him. While the Cat was still dangling in the air the Frenchman calmly stopped his motions with a well-placed pistol ball. Milfort's novel method of the coup de grace had been much discussed and was now known throughout the Confederacy as "Creek Murder."

In November Alex heard of Cornwallis' capitulation at Yorktown the month before. Now only the peace treaty remained to be signed and the evacuation of the British to be accomplished.

What did the Patriot victory bode for the Creek? Nothing good, surely, although much depended on whether or not in their treaty arrangements the British respected tribal titles to land and made provision for the trade that was so important to the Creek Nation. The Creek, like the other southern Indians, had become used to and could not do without the gun, the copper kettle, the steel knife, the European shirt and blanket. Not to mention European hard liquor.

Even if the British respected Indian tribal titles, the question arose as to whether the United States government would also, or the Georgians and South Carolinians who had already encroached across the eastern frontier.

The future looked far from bright. Meanwhile the Creeks could only wait until the peace treaty was signed, which would not be for some time, for the treaty must not only satisfy the chief signatories, the Americans and the British, but must also take into account Spanish conquests on the lower Mississippi and in the Floridas which had made Britain's position east of the Mississippi untenable.

Meanwhile, Alexander thought, he had best bestir himself in meeting the threat of William Bowles. With Milfort, Paro and a small guard he went to the Lower Creek town of Cussitahs, where Bowles was living, to meet the man and take his measure. But Bowles had left for the Bahamas and his pregnant wife had no idea when her husband would return.

By dint of judicious questioning Alex established that Bowles had gone to the Bahamas for the purpose of forming connections with wealthy merchants there in order to establish a Creek trade. Certainly the Marylander was in need of money and connections; his new warehouse was makeshift and quite empty of goods, and even lacked a watchman.

Milfort suggested that Alex burn the warehouse to the ground to repay Bowles for his insults at Pensacola and to discourage his return. But Alex had no desire to alienate Bowles's father-in-law, chief of Cussitahs, or to worsen the financial plight of his expectant wife. He even gave her enough money to buy some blankets needed for the winter.

Milfort disapproved of his generosity. "When Bowles returns," the Frenchman said, "and hears of your gift he will take it as evidence that you're afraid of him and want to curry his favor. This will only lead to more trouble."

"That's enough, Louis," Alex told his brother-in-law crisply. "I'm capable of making my own decisions."

He returned to Little Tallassie to find that a large American pack train had gone through the town on its way to the larger Creek towns of the area. This, and the fact of Bowles's departure for the Bahamas, made it imperative to begin on a definite course calculated to establish a Creek trade dominated not by Bowles but himself. For the man who dominated Creek trade would have the major voice in the formation of Creek policies.

With whom should the Creeks trade? The American traders were yet to prove their abilities and American manufactures were in a primitive state; moreover, he had not forgiven the Americans their persecution of his father. Although the Spaniards had never very satisfactorily supplied Creek trading needs, Pensacola was the most eligible town through which to supply the Creek Nation. Furthermore, trading relations between the Spanish and the Creeks would be valuable in cementing an alliance between Spain and the Creeks should Britain abandon the latter.

There was no time to lose. Although he had a touch of the fever, and Janine urged him to postpone the trip, Alex formed a small party and set out immediately for Pensacola to consult William Panton, who had traded with his father before the war. It was said that Panton had excellent connections with the Spanish.

Pensacola was attractively situated upon gentle, rising hills environing a harbor spacious enough to berth all the navies of Europe. On the east was the Bayou Texar and on the west the Bayou Chico, wide arms of the bay that reached inland on either side of the Pensacola Peninsula.

Several rivers ran into the great bay from the continent, dividing and spreading abroad their numerous branches over the expansive, flat low country which consisted of savannah and cane meadows. Along these rivers the higher land was rich, and here were many plantations producing indigo, rice and corn.

The names of streets were a heritage from the early Spanish settlers—Zarragossa, Palafox, Taragona, Intendenca. There were several hundred buildings in Pensacola, now a city far different in appearance than it had been in 1763, when Pensacola became a British colony and was made the capital of West Florida. At that time the town consisted of forty huts, thatched with palmetto leaves and barracks, the whole surrounded by a stockade of pine posts.

The governor's palace was a large stone building ornamented with a tower. The town was defended by Fort George, a large wooden stockade. Within the fortress was the council chamber where the records were kept, apartments for the officers, barracks, arsenal and magazines. There were several merchants and gentlemen who had buildings in the town.

William Panton's office and warehouse were on Garden Street, which during the British occupation had served as a community garden and pasture. At the outbreak of the Revolution Pensacola had become a haven for Tories. The most important commercial result of this immigration was the establishment of the Scotch firm of Panton, Leslie and Company. It was Panton's object to capture the Indian trade of West Florida, and he had succeeded; often Alex had heard his father speak highly of William Panton and predict that his fellow Scot would become the first millionaire in America.

Panton had emigrated from Scotland to Charles Town in 1742. For several years he was a member of the firm of Moore and Panton, of Savannah. At the outbreak of the Revolution he had moved to the more congenial atmosphere of East Florida, where he organized, with Thomas Forbes as his chief associate, the firm of Panton, Forbes and Company and built up trade and influence with the Creek Indians. His consistently Loyalist attitudes had brought him into conflict with the South Carolina and Georgia authorities, and early in the Revolution they had culminated in Panton's permanent outlawry by the Georgia Provincial Congress and the confiscation of his property.

After finding accommodations in Pensacola, Alex called on the trader. Obviously it was his father's name that gained him entrance to Panton's inner offices; the trader had never heard of Alexander McGillivray himself.

The stocky, shrewd-eyed Scot asked about Lachlan McGillivray's health and then sat silent, waiting for Alex to state his business. Alex told him that American traders were once again using the trading paths to the Creek Nation and that William Bowles had gone to Nassau to obtain backing. If Panton wished to cut them out, he had best move quickly to renew his relations with the Creek chiefs. The cooperation of Alex himself would be essential in this regard.

Panton smiled. "Mr. McGillivray, resentment of the Americans' treatment of your father cannot be the only reason why you are here. What would you yourself personally expect from an alliance with Panton and Leslie?"

"Financially, you mean?"

"Yes."

"Why, nothing. I would want only favors for my people."

Panton, the hardheaded businessman, did not believe him. "Oh, come, Mr. McGillivray, can you be as disinterested as all that?"

"This is the way I reason, sir, and I will be frank with you. I wish to guide the destinies of the Creek, for if I do not, I fear they will perish. An arrangement with Panton and Leslie would convince the Spanish that I hold sway in the Creek Nation. With Spanish patronage I could then establish ascendancy over the tribe. And I am interested in Spanish patronage for still another reason. If the British abandon the Indians, which seems increasingly probable, only from the Spanish can I obtain arms to protect my people from the Americans."

"Very neat," commented Panton, with a new look of respect on his bulldog face. "But you are making a number of assumptions. The first is that the English trader, any English trader, has a future in Spanish America. Did you know that Protestants have been ordered to leave St. Augustine and Pensacola?"

"I know Spain's erstwhile enemies are unpopular with them, Mr. Panton, but something tells me that you will be one of the few Englishmen to survive here. The Spanish have no experienced traders of their own, and they will find a way to use you."

Panton laughed. "I like you, sir. I like your intelligence, your resourcefulness and your ideas. I see for myself a financial opportunity if the Creeks become partial to Spain, assuming you can guarantee my operations complete safety. But first I must save my neck with the Spanish. Let us talk again when matters are somewhat clearer in this regard."

Alexander returned to Little Tallassie satisfied with the meeting. Panton wrote him an acknowledgment of it, and thereafter they corresponded regularly. Panton continued to remain in Pensacola, although other British traders in the Floridas closed up shop and sailed home. But, as the trader wrote, he still felt far from secure.

A new British cabinet agreed to recognize American independence in early 1782. A preliminary agreement was signed in Paris in November of that year and the treaty itself was signed in September, 1783.

Its provisions concerning the Creeks were precisely as Alex had feared. England had signed away Indian territory in the South with absolutely no regard for the boundaries observed for the red man. No effort was made to protect the English trader in the Spanish possessions.

The Creeks were in the most serious predicament of their history. With either the Spanish or the Americans, both recent adversaries, they must negotiate for recognition of Creek sovereignty and an effective trade.

Alex had predicted to the chiefs of the Creek Confederacy that the English would abandon them. He had discouraged response to a few tentative feelers from the Americans on the

grounds that the weak central government would be powerless to restrain either the land-hungry backwoodsmen of
Georgia and the Carolinas or the land speculators who had
begun to threaten Indian holdings. He had also urged an
understanding with Spain, whose possessions in America were
being endangered by the Americans. Spain's logical defense,
he said, would be to strengthen the Indian nations as buffers
against the expanding Americans.

He had encountered opposition. Opilth Mico, Mad Dog and
other chiefs did not share his view that the United States
had little chance to endure as a nation, and believed that the
central government would prevent serious depredations by
the backwoodsmen and settlers. The White Lieutenant, outstanding chief of the Lower Creeks, hated the Spaniards
because his only son had been killed by a Spanish bullet at
Pensacola. Some other chiefs wanted to trade with the Americans on the dubious theory that if trade relations were
strengthened between Georgia, the Carolinas and the Creeks,
then land encroachments would be less likely.

Alex did not bring up the matter of an election of a supreme chief to administer Creek affairs in the new crisis; the
chiefs were still too divided in their thinking to permit such
an election, which he hoped to win. What he needed to gain
authority in the Confederacy was definite Spanish support,
which would go far to negate the arguments of the small but
vocal anti-Spanish faction.

So far this support was nonexistent, but in the next
months, when the Creek Nation learned of the signing of a
treaty between England and Spain and the return of the
Floridas to Spain, Alexander, beginning with the new year
of 1784, started his campaign for Spanish protection and
trade in a series of letters to Arturo O'Neill, governor of
Pensacola.

Britain, he wrote, "had no right to transfer the Creek
Nation to any power whatever contrary to our inclination
and interest. We certainly as a free Nation have a right to

choose our protector, and what power is so fitting as the Master of the Floridas?"

He gave his reasons why it would be good policy for the Spanish Crown to go along with Creek interests. France had made a pressing demand for the return of its loan to the United States, and in order to raise the money Congress had laid heavy taxes on the thirteen states. As a result, a large number of people, together with a great number of disbanded soldiers, had left their homes to avoid the taxes and gone to seek new homes in the wilderness. Once these people were settled in the Indian territories it would be a difficult task to expel them.

Georgian and Carolinian traders, he went on, were making every effort to corner the Creek trade. Should they succeed in doing so they would use their influence in turning the Indians against Spain, and would make use of them in any designs they might form against Pensacola, Mobile and elsewhere.

He advised that several methods ought to be taken to frustrate the American schemes. A principal consideration was an active trade with the Creeks on the same scale as the English trade had been, "for Indians will attach themselves to those who best supply their necessities. If what I have written should meet with approbation by the Crown of Spain, the Crown will gain and secure a powerful barrier in these parts against the ambitions of the Americans. I likewise herewith beg leave to offer my services as an agent for Indian affairs on the part of his Most Catholic Majesty, in which capacity I have served his Brittanic Majesty for some years past." He signed the letter, "A Chief of the Creek Nation."

O'Neill replied quickly, suggesting a possible meeting in Pensacola between Alex, himself and Esteban Miró, governor of Louisiana. But although Alex replied in turn that he could come to Pensacola at O'Neill's convenience, there was no word from the governor for several months.

Alex suspected that O'Neill was gathering information on himself and his importance among the Creeks. William Panton confirmed this in a letter saying that O'Neill's aide had approached him for information and that the Spaniard had found it hard to believe that a Creek Indian could write such excellent English. Panton had spoken highly of Alexander. As for himself, Panton went on, he was grimly hanging on in Pensacola, using his influence with Spanish officials to prevent the fate that had befallen his British competitors in St. Augustine.

At the moment, Alex had other matters on his mind. Opilth Mico and a faction of white traders, who were in favor of an American trade, had chosen that moment to challenge his authority. Led by a Colonel Sullivan, they had gone so far as to plot his murder. The conspiracy came to light when one of the Creek members defected and came to Alex with the details of his intended assassination.

Alex moved quickly. Arresting parties led by himself, Milfort and Durant surrounded the houses of Sullivan and his chief lieutenants. No time was wasted; they were promptly executed in the public squares. Alex showed mercy to the dead men's families—they were allowed to stay on in the Nation if they chose, or to leave with sufficient funds to get them to Charles Town or Savannah. All elected to remain, and never once in succeeding years did they give him any trouble or seek revenge.

But it was a different situation with old Opilth Mico, who, with his entire Bear Clan, pronounced Alexander McGillivray a "boy and a usurper." To show his independence, Opilth promptly departed for the frontier to treat with various Georgia traders.

"Arrest the old man on his return," Louis Milfort advised, "and banish him from the country. You know his influence in the Lower Towns."

But Alexander believed the Bear Clan was too powerful

to come to death grips with at the moment. He contented himself with burning the old chief's houses in his absence and destroying his corn and cattle.

After Opilth's return a fire of mysterious origin broke out in the plantation outbuildings and was extinguished just in time. Several of Alex's cattle were poisoned. But there was no definite evidence that Opilth was the culprit, and so he could not take severer measures against him than he had.

In July Alex's letters to O'Neill bore fruit, and he was invited to visit Pensacola in September to meet with the governor and Miró. Miró was making a special trip from his New Orleans headquarters.

Like Arturo O'Neill, Estevan Rodriguez Miró was a soldier. During the American Revolution he had served in the West Florida campaigns as aide-de-camp to Bernardo de Galvez, and was rewarded with promotion to colonel. When Galvez left Louisiana in 1782, Miró was made acting governor. So far he had given Louisiana a mild and beneficent administration, encouraging commerce and agriculture, and opposing establishment of the dreaded Inquisition.

Alex had heard from William Panton that Miró loved dinner parties and was averse to hard work, most of which he loaded on his secretary. His first impression of the governor of Louisiana bore this out—Miró contented himself with drinking glass after glass of wine, and let O'Neill do all the talking.

"We have been much impressed with your letters," O'Neill opened the conversation. "It is unusual to find an Indian who writes English so well. Of course you were educated in the colonies?"

"Of course," replied Alex shortly. He wasn't going to allow these men, however important, to patronize him.

"The Crown has replied to our report on your suggestions and recommendations," said O'Neill. "We have been ordered to hold a meeting with the Creeks at Pensacola in June, and with the other southern tribes at Mobile, in August. Are these dates agreeable to you, and will you assist us in setting up the conferences?"

Alex nodded, hiding his elation. The first step of his master plan was achieved, and certainly the Spanish Crown now looked upon him as the chief representative of his nation.

"Are you prepared," O'Neill went on, "to give us your viewpoint on what articles should be included in a treaty of trade and peace between the Creek and the Spanish nations?"

"I am, Governor," Alex said and O'Neill motioned to his secretary to join them.

Alex outlined his recommendations, none of which he had discussed with any other Creek leaders but which he was fairly sure the chiefs would agree to, now that he was sure to be appointed an agent of the Spanish government. He said that the Creeks would wish their lands to be guaranteed in full by the Spaniards, not merely those Creek lands that fell within Spanish limits as set by the treaty between England and Spain. He asked for arms with which to resist American encroachments. He asked for equitable tariffs that would fully protect Creek products. He requested that William Panton, as the trader who could best supply Creek needs, be given a monopoly of the Creek trade at Pensacola and Mobile.

Miró put down his glass and spoke for the first time. "Colonel McGillivray," he said, using Alex's defunct British rank, "I must tell you now that you ask for too much. The Spanish do not wish for serious trouble with the Americans, and for that reason we cannot guarantee Creek territory not within our boundaries. Nor can we supply you with arms except for self-defense, or give William Panton a monopoly of the Indian trade. As for tariffs, I am sure they can be adjusted to our mutual satisfaction."

Alex had to admit he had underestimated Miró; the Spaniard spoke both clearly and forcefully, even though he had started on his second bottle of Madeira.

It was time to show some of the Creek teeth, thought Alex.

"Let us be frank, Governor," he said. "Both of us know that it is to the Spanish interest to destroy American influence with the tribes, lest the Americans incite us to harass the Spanish settlements or persuade us in any way to cooperate in the conquest of Louisiana and the Floridas. Let me tell you that American influence is strong. Now it is Spain's purpose to accomplish through trade what her diplomacy has failed to do, to erect the Southern Indian tribes into a barrier between the United States and the Spanish empire. I am willing to help you to erect that barrier, but my people must be helped to build it, too, and to do so they must be given arms and ammunition."

O'Neill was frowning. "You say American influence is strong among the Indians. Our agents have been able to find out little about it. Can you document your statement, Colonel?"

Alex found himself in a predicament. He could have mentioned Opilth Mico's visit to the Georgians, from which the old chief had returned with little or nothing accomplished, but the fact that Opilth Mico was from Little Tallassie, supposedly dominated by Alexander McGillivray, was not a fact that would add to the prestige of Alexander McGillivray among the Spaniards. He did not bring up Opilth, but mentioned instead the appearance in the Lower Creek towns of various Georgian traders, and the matter of William Bowles, of which the Spanish were completely ignorant. Their agents must be poor indeed.

This information appeared to impress O'Neill, but Miró was unaffected by it. "I will repeat, Colonel," he said, "we do not wish a war with the United States over Creek boundaries. We will help the Creeks to defend themselves against American encroachments, but not to provoke the Americans."

Miró was firmly committed to a defensive policy against the Americans, thought Alex, and there would be no budging him. The amount of arms and ammunition to be received by the Creeks from the Spanish would be a ticklish matter; better drop it for the present.

"You say you cannot give William Panton a monopoly of the Creek trade," he said. "May I inquire as to why?"

"I am not at liberty to answer your question at the moment," said Miró evasively. "But perhaps we would be able to confirm Panton in his trading privileges at St. Marks."

"The only way," said Alex, "to guarantee the loyalty of the Creeks is to see that they are well supplied. Panton and Leslie is the wealthiest trading house in the South, and the most efficient."

In answer Miró poured himself another glass of wine, and O'Neill put in quickly, "We are recommending a commission for you as colonel and a salary of thirty-five dollars a month. I hope this is satisfactory."

Alex nodded. The salary was small. To convince him that he had bargained well, the Spaniards would probably increase it before the signing of the treaty. After the conference he called on William Panton. The trader thought he knew why Miró had not wanted to discuss the question of a monopoly of the Creek trade for Panton and Leslie; there were rumors that he and Martin Novarro, a high Louisiana official, had already promised the privilege to a New Orleans firm in which they had a financial interest. "However, I'm glad Miró mentioned confirming me at St. Marks," Panton said. "With a toehold one can start scrambling up the bank. Alexander, I think you have saved me, and I am grateful."

After three days of talks with the Spaniards, Alexander returned to Little Tallassie to learn that the Creek chiefs, in his absence, had received a Georgian invitation to Augusta to discuss an agreement for an American trade. He had gone to Pensacola just in time.

He called a conference to be held at Coweta in three weeks. The conference was a personal triumph for Alexander McGillivray. His strategy had been successful; now that the

Spaniards had accepted him as spokesman of the Nation the Creek chiefs, with few exceptions, followed suit. They commended him for his diplomacy. They agreed that the Creeks could not expect Spanish guarantee of all their lands, nor, at the moment, substantial Spanish arms with which to stay the encroachments of the Americans. They voted unanimously to decline the Georgian invitation for trade discussions. Back in Little Tallassie, Alex wrote, as spokesman for his Nation, to the leading chiefs of the Choctaw and the Chickasaw, informing them of the treaty conference in Mobile with the Spanish in July.

He had not expected Spanish concessions before the meeting in June, and there were none. Trading privileges with the Creeks were given to the New Orleans firm of Mather and Strother, although Panton was allowed to do business in St. Marks. The two-day meeting was concluded with the signing of the treaty and the tariff prices. His own salary as commissary for the Creeks was increased from thirty-five to fifty dollars a month.

In the seventeen months following the Treaty of Pensacola Alexander McGillivray found his lot and that of his people to be a happy one. The wisdom of the Spanish alliance had been demonstrated by the fact that, except in the Cumberland, American encroachments had ceased, at least for the present. The credit of William Panton's trading competitor was found wanting and Panton was slowly but surely taking over the Indian trade, to his profit and that of the Creeks. The standing of Alexander McGillivray with his own people had never been higher. His domestic life—he had a devoted wife, a delightful infant son, with another child on the way —was happy.

"My position is an enviable one," he wrote to Governor O'Neill. "I would rather remain governor of my savages than change places with the King of England or the President of the United States."

VIII

"WE WANT NOTHING FROM YOU BUT JUSTICE"

Charleston
10 June 1785

To the Kings, Headmen and Warriors of the Creeks

FRIENDS & BROTHERS

The war being over the United States in Congress assembled have ordered their swords to be sheathed, and they have appointed three of their trusty and beloved men to meet you, the kings, headmen and warriors of the Creek Nation, to treat with you for the purpose of making peace with you and receiving you into their favor and protection and for removing between us all causes of future contention and quarrels.

FRIENDS

We are the three beloved men and according to the power given us we have appointed Galphinton on the River Ogeechee to be the place where we will meet you on the 24th day of October next. We shall provide provisions and other things proper for your accommodation.

FRIENDS

The United States of America are a great and brave Nation. They have a great many warriors and have conquered all their enemies, and are now desirous of peace with all the world. They remember you were once their friends and they intend to forget that you were their enemies in the late war. But you must forget it also, and we will take you by the hand.

                    BENJAMIN HAWKINS
                    ANDREW PICKENS
                    JOSEPH MARTIN *

* From *McGillivray of the Creeks*, by John Walton Caughey. Copyright 1938 by the University of Oklahoma Press.

Alexander McGillivray found this letter amusing. The Americans had not given up hopes of persuading the Creeks to abandon their Spanish alliance. And they were going about persuading them to do so in a foolish way, with rhetoric and patronizing verbiage.

He would have expected something more intelligent from such outstanding men as Benjamin Hawkins and Andrew Pickens. Hawkins, a North Carolinian, was a graduate of the College of New Jersey. During the war he had been a member of Washington's staff, and later a Congressman. Pickens, one of the outstanding partisan fighters of the war, was respected by the Indians for his understanding of their ways. Did these men know no better than to address Alexander McGillivray as if he were a credulous savage?

His reply to Pickens, in its ease and polish, was meant to embarrass the commissioners and put them in their places.

Little Tallassie
5 September 1785

Sir: I am favored by your letter by Brandon who, after detaining it near a month, sent it by an Indian a few days ago.

The notification you have sent us is agreeable to our wishes, as the meeting is intended for the desirable purpose of adjusting and settling matters, on an equitable footing, between the United States and the Creek Nation. At the same time, I cannot avoid surprise that a measure of this nature should have been so long delayed. At American Independence we expected that the new government would have taken some steps to make up the differences that subsisted between them and the Indians during the war; to have taken them under their protection, and confirmed to them their hunting grounds.

Such a course would have reconciled the minds of the Indians and secured the State their friendship. The Georgians, whose particular interest it was to conciliate the friend-ship of this Nation, have acted in all respects to the contrary. I am sorry to observe that violence and prejudice have taken the place of good policy and reason in all their proceed-ings with us. Their talks with us breathe nothing but ven-geance, and being entirely possessed with the idea that we were wholly at their mercy, they never once reflected that the colonies of a powerful monarch nearly surrounded us to whom, in an extremity, we might apply for succor and pro-tection.

How the boundary and limits between the Spaniards and the States will be determined a little time will show. We shall pay no attention to any limits that may prejudice our claims that were drawn by an American and confirmed by a British negotiator. Yet, notwithstanding that we have been obliged to adopt these measures for our preservation, we sincerely wish to have it in our power to be on the same foot-ing with the States as before the late unhappy war, to effect which is entirely in your power. We want nothing from you but justice. We want our hunting grounds preserved from encroachments. They have been ours from the beginning of time and I trust that, with the assistance of our friends, we shall be able to maintain them against every attempt that may be made to take them from us.

To convince you of my sincere desire to restore a good understanding between us, I have taken the necessary steps to prevent any future predatory excursions of my people against any of your settlements. I could wish the people of Cumberland showed an equal good disposition to do what is right. They were certainly the first aggressors since the peace, and acknowledged it in a written certificate left at the Indian camp they had plundered.

I have only to add that we shall meet the commissioners of Congress whenever we shall receive notice in expectation that every matter of difference will be settled with that liberality and justice worthy of the men who have so gloriously asserted the cause of liberty and independence, and that we shall, in future, consider them as brethren, and defenders of the land.

    I am, with much respect, sir,
       Your obedient servant,
        ALEXANDER McGILLIVRAY

It was a masterly performance, firm in its insistence on the rights of his people, putting the Americans on notice that any further encroachments in the Cumberland would be met with a defensive retaliation for which only the Americans could be blamed, and presenting the commissioners with a set of questions they would be hard pressed to answer with any confidence. Finally, it did not neglect to note that the commissioner had chosen to select a horse thief, Brandon, as the deliverer of their letter.

Alexander McGillivray chose not to show up for the conference at Galphinton. Only two Creek chiefs and a few warriors did. The angry commissioners refused to enter into any treaty with so inadequate a representation of the Creek towns. But the Georgians, also on hand, by means of threats and outright deception, were quick to sign a treaty which they claimed was completely legal.

This treaty confirmed the Treaty of Augusta of 1783, and granted to the state of Georgia the territory lying on the east side of a line to run from the juncture of the Oconee and Okmulgee rivers to the St. Mary's River, including all the islands and harbors, and constituting more than half the coast of Georgia.

The commissioners were more successful with the other southern Indians than they had been with the Creeks. In November large delegations of Cherokees, Choctaws and Chickasaws conferred with them on the Keowee River. Although they had already professed allegiance to Spain at the Mobile congress, these chiefs could not resist the American presents and signed a similar compact with the United States on terms disadvantageous to them.

Fresh from his triumph, Commissioner Hawkins lost no time in reporting it to the troublesome Creek spokesman, and asked, when he had "leisure and opportunity," to let him know why the Creeks had been so poorly represented at Galphinton. There was a threatening note in Hawkins' concluding words: "The Creeks alone seem blind to their own interest, and seem still desirous of provoking new troubles."

In writing of Hawkins' letter to O'Neill, Alexander commented: "The Americans all agree on one point: that it is my fault that they can't bring their schemes to bear with the Indians, and on that account their attention is engaged in contriving the manner in which they can bring about my assassination." * By "Americans" he did not mean Benjamin Hawkins or Andrew Pickens, but certain Georgians whom he had heard were plotting his death.

Georgian encroachments were proceeding apace. Georgians were settling on the Oconee and Alabama rivers, and on the Tennessee River at a place called Muscle Shoals. Settlers were flocking into the Cumberland area and even moving towards the Mississippi.

In excuse of these depredations they cited the shameful Augusta Conference of 1783 and the spurious "grants" they had extracted from straggling Indian hunters who had no idea of the documents to which they were putting their marks.

In March, 1786 Alexander called a general convention of the Creek Nation to consider the question of American aggressions. The convention was held a month later.

---

* From *McGillivray of the Creeks,* by John Walton Caughey. Copyright 1938 by the University of Oklahoma Press.

It was clear, he told the assembled chiefs, that war was the only alternative left the Creeks to force the Georgians to abandon their encroachments. Now that the Creeks were allied with the great and powerful nation of Spain, they had the means to defend "lands that our Fathers have owned and possessed ever since the first rising of the sun and the flowing of the waters."

The Congress of the United States, he said, must be acquitted of any designs against the Creek; the state of Georgia was acting in opposition to its recommendations. It was the obligation of the Creeks to check the Georgians before they became too strong for the Creeks to deal with them.

However, bloodshed on the part of the Creek warriors was neither necessary nor desirable. Such bloodshed would only call down retaliation upon the Nation's head. It was his recommendation that the settlers merely be driven off the lands they had usurped, and their buildings destroyed. Warriors were to use their weapons only in self-defense.

The recommendations of the "Beloved Man," as he now was called, were accepted unanimously. Parties of warriors were sent out in every direction wherever the Americans had already settled or were forming new settlements in Creek territory. The Oconee lands were cleared of usurpers and Louis Milfort led an expedition to Cumberland. Here, due to the large number of inhabitants, the warriors could not drive them off entirely, although the settlers' plantations and cabins were destroyed after they had taken refuge in their stockades. There were, inevitably, a few white casualties, due to the extreme hatred and rancor the people bore towards the Indians. At Muscle Shoals the Creek warriors found only a few building foundations which they destroyed.

To protect the frontier, Colonel Elijah Clarke marched to the Oconee with one hundred and fifty men, but found the Creeks under Milfort in such large numbers that he was forced to retreat and send for reinforcements. These arrived too late to prevent the clearing of the Oconee country, or to allow for a clash between Milfort's men and Clarke's troops, from the Indian point of view a fortunate circumstance.

Although Alex had informed the Spanish governors at Pensacola, New Orleans and St. Augustine of the April conference, and written that he had no intention of precipitating raids against the Georgians without Spanish concurrence, the fact remained that he had not waited for their approval. This had been deliberate on his part. His purpose was to test his strength and obtain long-overdue arms and ammunition from the reluctant Spaniards.

His strategy bore fruit. Zespedes, governor of St. Augustine, praised the "unexampled moderation" the Creeks had shown in driving off the encroachers with a minimum of violence. The Creeks, he said, were fully justified in repelling invasion by defensive means. He promised a quantity of powder and ball for "hunting." O'Neill promptly sent a certain amount of military stores. Only Miró was reluctant to risk embarrassment with the United States government, and forbade O'Neill to promise McGillivray ammunition in writing. He invited the Creek chief to New Orleans for "discussions" in May.

Louis Milfort doubted that Alexander could convince the governor of Louisiana that it was to the Spanish interest to arm the Creeks against the Georgians. "Miró almost certainly has orders from the Spanish court," cautioned the Frenchman. "Your trip will be useless."

"Useless or not, I am going," Alex told him.

From Pensacola Alex traveled to New Orleans by boat. It was the first time he had visited the Louisiana capital, set in a semitropical country surrounded by swamps and low-lying delta lands.

New Orleans had been founded about 1718 by the Sieur de Beinville, who with French engineers cleared the land and plotted the city along a curve of the Mississippi at a point

UNDER MY WINGS EVERY THING PROSPERS

New Orleans, late in the 18th century

where the river swings nearest the Bayou St. John and Lake Pontchartrain.

The new settlement, named in honor of the Duc d'Orleans, Regent of France, superseded Biloxi as the capital of the vast colonial empire of Louisiana. At that early date it was a mere outpost housing officials, soldiers, merchants, slaves and rivermen. During the ten-year administration of the Marquis de Vaudreuil, who took office in 1743, New Orleans became a gay social center, imitative of Versailles.

Following the partition of Louisiana between Spain and England in 1763, New Orleans was named the capital of Spanish Louisiana. Its citizens, angered by the transfer, received hostilely the commissioner sent to establish Spanish authority. Revolt brewed for two years. In 1768 a petition was circulated demanding the commissioner's expulsion. Guns at the city gates were spiked on the night of October 27 and the next day a mob of four hundred Acadians, Germans, settlers and other insurgents took over the city. The commissioner sailed for Cuba, and New Orleans became the first colonial capital to revolt against European rule.

Its independence was short-lived. In August, 1768 Count Alexander O'Reilly, with twenty-four ships and more than two thousand men, arrived at New Orleans. No opposition was offered by the town and next day, to the shouts of "Viva el Rey!" and the thunder of cannon, the flag of Spain was raised in the Plaza de Armas.

Another Irish soldier, Major Enrique White, who had cast his lot with the Spaniards, was Alex's personal host in the capital. The Creek leader was put up in an elegant house near the French quarter, and told that Governor Miró would meet with him next day, after he had rested from his trip.

Alex's approach with Miró was different from when they had last met in Pensacola. This time he attacked immediately, with a demand for 7,500 pounds of powder and 15,000 pounds of ball, together with guns, flints and other military supplies.

Miró was dumbfounded. "Surely, Colonel, you cannot be serious. You are asking for a mountain of material!"

"We need every bit of it, your Excellency. Have you heard of the Georgian plans to invade the Creek country and destroy my tribe?"

"They are only rumors," Miró protested. "I cannot conceive of such a thing happening."

"Then you should consult the Georgian temper, as I have. Your Excellency, are we allies, bound by solemn covenant, or are we not?"

Miró could not withstand Alex's verbal onslaught. Finally he agreed to 5,000 pounds of powder and 10,000 pounds of ball, precisely what Alex had been bargaining for by demanding a larger amount. But Miró insisted that the ammunition could be delivered only if Colonel McGillivray could find some indirect way of getting it into the hands of his warriors. Under no circumstances must the Americans obtain evidence of its Spanish origin.

Alex found a way to satisfy Miró's caution. The ammunition could be delivered to his warehouse at Little Tallassie. The braves would come for it there only at night, and with no more than two horses at a time. In this way lurking Georgian agents would be unlikely to notice the transactions. In every case a receipt in his name would serve as clearance. Alex left New Orleans with assurances that the ammunition would begin to leave Pensacola for Little Tallassie within two weeks' time.

His journey homeward was a difficult one. He contracted a fever on the way from Pensacola, and for the last fifty miles was carried in an improvised litter. For a week he was in bed. Not until he was on his feet again and taking regular nourishment did Louis Milfort tell him about the difficulties that Daniel McMurphy, a Georgian agent, had caused in his absence. McMurphy evidently had information of his New Orleans trip. He had arrived in Little Tallassie the day after Alex left it.

"It was plain the fellow was up to no good," reported Milfort, "and I would have sent him packing immediately had it not been for your orders that no stranger is to be refused the hospitality of the town."

With great arrogance McMurphy had called together the principal traders of the Upper Creeks at Coweta, saying that he was empowered to issue them trading licenses approved by the state of Georgia, after which the traders would be responsible only to him. The traders had laughed in his face, replying that they held licenses from Alexander McGillivray and needed no others. That night, intending to give him a scare, the traders had dressed as Creek warriors and attacked McMurphy's lodge, sending the night-shirted Georgian fleeing into the woods. By sunrise he was on his way back to Augusta.

Alex marveled at the Georgian lack of tact and diplomacy, for they chose this inauspicious moment to appoint a group of commissioners to try to negotiate a cession to Georgia of the disputed Oconee River lands. Their letter of mid-August inviting the Creeks to a conference on the Oconee in October, piously protesting a desire for peace at the same time as it threatened warfare should the Creeks prove unaccommodating, was particularly annoying to Alex.

Alex had no hesitation in replying that no useful purpose would be served by a conference until evacuation of the Indian lands occupied by the settlers since the Treaty of 1773 was accomplished. He demanded that all settlers leave the Oconee lands within a month's time. He felt on firm ground; Spain had now delivered arms and ammunition and stood firmly behind the Nation in the Oconee crisis.

It was a measure of his still incomplete authority that two Creek chiefs, the Fat King and Tame King, stubbornly insisted upon attending the Georgian conference. They came to regret it. The Georgians imprisoned both men and their parties and held them as hostages to force the Nation as a whole to capitulate.

Alexander McGillivray was unmoved. In reply to notification of the arrests he said that anyone who had always professed friendship for the Americans who were now using them so badly, might stay with them as long as they wished.

At this point the hapless Daniel McMurphy again reentered the picture, accompanying to the Creek Nation the two chiefs who had now been released, although five of their attendants were still being held by the Georgians.

McMurphy carried with him a threat from his state government. Unless the Creeks agreed forthwith to meet with the American commissioners, militiamen would be sent to Creek country to arrest all their important leaders.

Alexander smiled at the none-too-bright Georgian. "Under whose command will these troops be?" he asked.

"Under the command of General Twigs and Governor Samuel Elbert."

"Former Governor Elbert of Savannah?" asked Alex.

"The same."

"I see. Well, you tell Governor Elbert that he had best be as good a soldier as he is a thief, or he will leave Creek country minus his scalp." He would never forget that his ex-employer had been one of the men who had "bought" Lachlan McGillivray's holdings for two shillings to the pound.

Although he was in Little Tallassie as an envoy of his state, McMurphy had the poor taste and worse sense to approach the Creek brave delegated as his guide and factotum with a bribe to murder his host. The offer, four wagonloads of goods, was promptly reported to the Beloved Man.

Alexander waited until shortly before dawn of the next morning. Then, carrying a horsewhip, he appeared at McMurphy's lodge.

For the second time the Georgian was routed out of bed in his night shirt and sent on his way. "Give your masters this message," Alex told him. "All they accomplish by sending men of your witlessness to eliminate me is to insult my intelligence. If you are the best that Georgia has her cause is plainly futile."

The Georgia invasion was deferred. In September a representative from the Cumberland arrived in Little Tallassie soliciting a peace on any terms and conditions agreeable to the Creeks. Alex wanted to avoid an attack on the Nation from two directions simultaneously, east from Georgia and north from the Cumberland. Moreover he had kept his warriors under arms during the past summer, and in consequence they had been unable to hunt for their families. He consented to a truce with the Tennesseans until the following April. By that time Miró and O'Neill might receive advice from the Spanish court concerning final settlement of the limits between Spain and the United States, and on the basis of this he could act with Cumberland accordingly.

In December there was good news from William Panton.

Due largely to Alex's prestige and his unwearying solicitation of the Spanish on Panton and Leslie's behalf, the Scots trader had been granted what amounted to a monopoly of the Creek trade. The effect of this was to persuade most of those Creek chiefs who had associations with Georgia traders to terminate them in favor of working with the victor in the competition for the Nation's trade. As a side effect, American influence in the Nation was generally lessened.

In the spring Alexander convened two major meetings, the first at Coweta of the Lower Town chiefs, and the second, at Tuckabatches, of the Northern Indian nations. Present at the Coweta meeting was James White, a United States commissioner appointed by Congress to treat with the Creeks. The Beloved Man greeted White cordially; he was always more willing to talk with a representative of the federal government than with one representing Georgia. He told White that he was welcome to attend the meeting and address the chiefs. He also suggested that the Creeks be admitted as a separate state to the Union, an idea which obviously embarrassed the commissioner.

Alexander knew he had nothing to fear from White. His position was too insecure. The Georgians had briefed him badly, and he had convinced the commissioner that the various treaties entered into by dissident and nonrepresentative Creek chiefs were illegal. He had also persuaded him how vital it was to the Creeks to keep their hunting grounds. White therefore could not propose measures based on the Georgian point of view, and so contented himself with attacking the Spanish. He claimed that the Spaniards were hatching plots to subdue both the states and the Indians. The Indians should therefore join with the Americans in the defense of their country.

Louis Milfort turned nervously to Alexander. "Should you allow him to go on this way?"

"Why not?" Alex smiled. "When the Spanish hear of

White's speech, and I shall see to it that they do, they'll redouble their efforts to retain Creek loyalty. White cannot hurt us; he can only help."

When the American commissioner was finished the chief of Coweta spoke eloquently for the Creeks, saying that while they had respect for the Congress' integrity, there was a third party involved, Georgia, who had no mind to do justice. "Our lands are our life and breath," the chief concluded. "If we part with them we part with our blood. We must fight for them, for there is no wilderness behind us to which we can retreat."

White left Coweta, his mission a failure. But it had served at least one purpose: clarifying for the United States government the real issues between the Creeks and Georgia. White reported to Congress that McGillivray's alliance with the Spanish had been beneficial to the Creeks; they were strong, independent and in a good position, in the event of conflict with the Georgians, to defeat them and maintain their boundaries. He described Alexander McGillivray as "the unrivaled spokesman of his people and a man of the highest intellectual stature and abilities. In diplomacy he has the artfulness of a Talleyrand."

IX

"I CAN ONLY CONTINUE ON"

Little Tallassie
20 June 1787

His Excellency, Governor Arturo O'Neill

Sir: I wish to inform you that we have had a great meeting with the chiefs of the Northern Nations, the Iroquois, Hurons, Mohawks, Wyandots, Oneidas and Shawnees. They came from the Northern Confederacy, consisting of twenty-five Nations, which inhabit the Lakes, the Ohio and Wabash rivers, and other parts of the western country of North America. I have concluded matters with them to serve the King's interest.

The Northerners tell me that they have routed and dispersed many parties of surveyors from the Ohio and western country, and we have agreed jointly to attack the Americans in every place wherever they shall pass over our own proper limits, nor ever to grant them lands, nor suffer their surveyors to roam about the country. They are now gone back, but another deputation is to arrive here in November next, to let us know how affairs come in the northward.

I had written to your Excellency some time ago requesting another addition to our ammunition. We have at least eight hundred warriors who have received none. To this letter you made no reply. The particular situation of our affairs makes a repetition of such a request absolutely necessary. I had informed you in a former letter that the Tallassies and Cussitahs and others of our Georgian Indian friends had come over to our interest, and that they ought to have ammunition. Yesterday an express arrived from the Cussitahs informing me that the Georgians had barbarously murdered six of their men without any cause whatever. These Indians were killed hunting for Americans. I have been at great pains to inculcate ideas and sentiments of humanity in the minds of the Indians, but such proceedings of the Americans thoroughly frustrate my good intentions.

This last stroke and insult offered to us by these people deserves the severest chastisement, which they shall certainly receive in due time.*

O'Neill had not forgotten to answer Alex's letter asking for ammunition. His omission had been deliberate. In the Spanish view the Creeks were waging war against the Georgians and the Cumberland settlers with entirely too much enthusiasm and rather alarming success. Alexander McGillivray had ended the truce between the Creeks and Cumberland without notifying the Spanish authorities, and in the last few weeks the Creeks had killed thirty-one Georgian frontiersmen and put the town of Greensboro, in Greene County, to the torch. Creek warriors were now fighting an offensive rather than a defensive war; the governor of Georgia had already protested to O'Neill and Miró against their aid to McGillivray and his aroused Indians. Nor were the Spaniards pleased that the Beloved Man had met with the chiefs of the Northern Confederacy without consulting with them on the agenda. They had concluded that McGillivray was becoming so powerful in his nation that he might bring about its complete independence. Spain wanted the Creek Nation dependent on the Crown.

Temporizing, O'Neill wrote that he awaited instructions from Governor Miró on new supplies of ammunition. It

* From *McGillivray of the Creeks,* by John Walton Caughey. Copyright 1938 by the University of Oklahoma Press.

was not until January, 1788 that Miró wrote direct, saying that Spanish support was to be diminished, giving no very definite reason for the decision. Alexander wrote immediately to Governor Zespedes of St. Augustine, detailing the Creeks's recent successes.

> "My warriors are victorious in every quarter over the Americans. The people of Cumberland are driven over the Ohio River and the State of Georgia now lies at our mercy. The Seminoles of Florida have agreed to join us, their brothers. When there is so good a prospect of compelling the Americans to relinquish all idea of their encroachments, I am at a loss to understand why Spain would suddenly deprive us of the means of achieving such a result."

He asked Zespedes for his good offices in obtaining a reply from Miró.

In June Alex received a letter from Andrew Pickens and George Matthews, naming themselves commissioners of Georgia and South Carolina and proposing that he name a date to discuss a settlement of the Oconee issue. Now that Spanish support was lacking—Miró had replied unfavorably to Zespedes' letter—Alex could not answer in as strong a manner as he wished. He suggested a meeting the following September, and promised a suspension of hostilities up to that time, but insisted on an evacuation of the Creek lands as a requisite preliminary to peace.

The American proposal prompted him to a stronger appeal to the Spaniards for renewed support. The effect of a desertion would, he said, be severe. "If it is the Royal will that we must make peace even at the sacrifice of all these lands which were the principal object of the war, in that case we shall consider ourselves as a ruined nation, to shift for ourselves." Miró did not respond to this open threat to scrap the Treaty of Pensacola.

In late June Alex received word from one of the Lower

Towns that a young Englishman had arrived with a present of powder and ball sent by a charitable society in England sympathetic to the Creek cause. The fact that the report came from the area in which William Bowles had lived before going to the Bahamas excited his suspicions, but he determined to meet with the generous stranger. To be on the safe side he took Milfort and a bodyguard of braves.

The stranger did indeed turn out to be Bowles. The adventurer was tanned and fit from his long sojourn in the Bahamas. He thanked his visitor for his kindness to his wife on his last visit to Cussitahs. He admitted that he had come not from England but from Nassau, where his backers were Lord Dunmore, the last colonial governor of Virginia and now governor of the Bahamas, and John Miller, of the firm of Miller and Bonamy. So charming was the Marylander, with his crooked grin and expansive manner of speech, that Alexander had to remind himself that this was the opportunist who had so ruthlessly attempted to replace him in the affections of his people.

"Let me guess your motives," Alex told him. "Dunmore and Miller plan to invade William Panton's trading monopoly, and think they can bribe me with this gift of powder and ball, and the Indians with presents, to reduce Panton's influence in favor of Miller and Bonamy."

Bowles flashed his brilliant smile. "You're close to the mark, Colonel, but not precisely on it. Dunmore and Miller hate the Spaniards. Both were practically ruined by them when they attacked Nassau in '82. They would do anything to embarrass Miró and Madrid."

"Come now, Captain—or is it General?—Messrs. Dunmore and Miller realize that any ammunition given to me will be used against the Americans to Spanish profit. You had better tell me the truth."

"Well, they want Panton's trade and they want to embarrass the Spanish," Bowles said, and rose to get another bottle of the excellent brandy he had brought with him from Nassau.

Alex pondered. He badly needed the ammunition Bowles had brought, which was considerable; without it, the Georgians and Cumberlanders might well turn on the Creeks and exact immediate revenge. Panton, of course, would be furious, but the Scotsman had done little or nothing to help persuade Miró and O'Neill to relax their current policy of noncooperation. The Spaniards must be shown that if they broke their promises he would seek help elsewhere. And finally, realistically speaking, Bowles had very little chance of destroying Panton's well-organized and efficient monopoly.

"What are your immediate plans?" Alex asked the adventurer when he had come back to the room.

"I must return to the Bahamas for more Indian presents."

The Indian trade would not be won by Bowles when he had few gifts for his prospective customers. "I accept your offer, Captain, and with thanks," Alex told him.

He returned to Little Tallassie with a personal gift from Bowles—a charming landscape of the Creek country painted by the talented Marylander. But no sooner had he begun to be more comfortable in his mind about the American threat because of Bowles's military supplies, than a new problem presented itself—that of regaining the confidence of Panton and the Spaniards.

Panton was furious at his acceptance of Bowles's gift, his anger inhibited only by the fact that Alexander had never profited personally from an association that had saved Panton with the Spanish and made him a tremendously wealthy man. The Spaniards investigated Bowles and decided that his purpose was to prevent peace between Georgia and the Creeks, and eventually, to recapture the Floridas for Great Britain. O'Neill was of the opinion that the Beloved Man of Little Tallassie had abandoned Spain and its interests and recommended that he be dropped as commissary and his commission be rescinded. Although unwilling to go that far, Miró and Zespedes were patently disturbed.

In November Bowles returned to Florida from Nassau with thirty-odd men, a few brass cannon and a few bolts of cloth. Shortly after they had landed, twenty-six of the crew deserted to the Spanish. With four villainous cutthroats and a few horseloads of goods, the crestfallen adventurer made his way to the Creek Nation.

The Indians were disappointed by his gifts and resentful of his arrogant, swaggering henchmen. His plan of supplanting Panton and Leslie temporarily stalled, Bowles began to curry favor with the Georgian traders. He claimed that neither Spain nor the United States had any right to control the Indians, that England had never ceded their country to either of these powers and that Alexander McGillivray had attempted to sell his people to the Spaniards. Reports reached Little Tallassie that Bowles was winning over certain Lower Town chiefs with a combination of Georgian goods and his magnetic charm.

Louis Milfort suggested for the second time that the adventurer be either forcibly expelled from the Nation or eliminated.

"None of your 'Creek Murders,' Louis," said Alex. "Bowles is becoming so objectionable now that the Spanish will find a way to take care of him."

He was, in any event, concerned with more crucial matters. North Carolina frontiersmen had burned several Indian villages, and in retaliation he had dispatched a war party under Charles Weatherford, as a result of which the Americans had retreated from the country. He had concluded another truce with the people of Cumberland, who had offered him a lot and buildings in Nashville and the honor of enrolling his name among their citizens. (He refused.) He had met with United States Commissioners Pickens and Matthews, although nothing more had been accomplished than the appointing of a meeting for June, 1789. This, however, had its advantages for the Creeks, for Pickens and Matthews were marking time until the Constitution should be adopted, at which time the new government was expected to formulate a more liberal Indian policy.

Gradually relations improved with the Spanish, and by April they had resumed the supplies of arms and ammunition. It was for this reason that Alex changed his plans for meeting with Pickens and Matthews in the spring. Such a meeting, he wrote the Americans, could not be productive; there had been too many recent and indeed current instances of hostilities between the Lower Creeks and the Georgians.

Unknown to Alexander McGillivray, the United States government in New York was giving serious attention to the Creek problem. Secretary of War Knox had prepared for President Washington a careful analysis of the advisability of a war with the difficult tribe, and had suggested ways of settling the outstanding issues. Washington leaned heavily on this report in his message to Congress, which approved it. In August, 1789, three new Indian commissioners—Benjamin Lincoln, David Humphreys and Cyrus Griffin—were given instructions based on Knox's ideas and suggestions and ordered to proceed immediately to the Oconee country to write a treaty between the Creeks and the state of Georgia.

The new commissioners were by far the most distinguished to have been entrusted with the task of negotiating with the elusive Alexander McGillivray.

Benjamin Lincoln had been a major general in the Continental army. At Saratoga he prepared the way for victory by breaking the enemy line of communication with Canada, and was severely wounded in the fighting against Burgoyne. Appointed to the command of the American army in the southern department, he had been captured in 1779 by Clinton in Charleston. Lincoln took part in the Yorktown campaign, and was delegated by Washington to receive

Major General Benjamin Lincoln

Cornwallis' sword. In 1781 he was made Secretary of War by Congress, a post which he held for two years.

In 1786 Benjamin Lincoln was named one of Massachusetts' commissioners to treat with the Penobscot Indians of Maine concerning land purchases. The following year he made his famous night march through a terrible snowstorm to Petersham, New Hampshire, where he brought Daniel Shay's Whisky Rebellion to a close; two years later he was chosen a member of the convention to consider the new Federal Constitution, and worked for its ratification.

Colonel David Humphreys

David Humphreys was a soldier, statesman and poet. During the Revolution, as an officer in a Connecticut militia regiment, he had begun a lifelong devotion to George Washington that won him the title "Beloved of Washingon." His record in the war had been a brilliant one, and at twenty-eight he was a lieutenant-colonel. In his well-known *The Life of Israel Putnam,* he wrote as he fought, coolly and vigorously.

Humphreys had appeared in paintings of Washington's general staff, and celebrated him in verse; he was a frequent visitor at Mount Vernon. He had spent two years in France and England on diplomatic work for Franklin, Adams and Jefferson. Elected in 1786 a member of the Assembly of Connecticut, in the same year he was appointed commandant of a new regiment against the Indians on the middle western frontier. He had a reputation of being overbearing, pompous and an execrable poet, but he was considered both able and tireless.

Cyrus Griffin was a statesman, jurist and the last president of Congress. In 1782 he had been one of the judges chosen by the states of Connecticut and Pennsylvania to preside over the provisional court that determined ownership of the Wyoming Valley, and his services in settling that important controversy led President Washington to appoint him, along with Lincoln and Humphreys, to attend the Creek-Georgia treaty. Griffin was accomplished and upright, dependable and industrious.

The commissioners sailed from New York on August 31, reached Savannah on September 10, and set out immediately for Rock Landing on the Oconee with a party of four hundred troops, arriving five days later. Alexander McGillivray and his party of chiefs and warriors, numbering nine hundred, arrived at Rock Landing the following day.

A series of mutual visits between the white and Indian camps began. At the Creek camp the ceremony of the black drink was observed with great formality.

The black drink was a decoction of the leaves and tender shoots of the Cassine. Following its brewing, bundles of dry cane, previously split and broken in pieces to the length of two feet, were placed obliquely crossways upon one another on the floor of the meeting tent, forming a spiral circle around the tent's central pillar. This circle extended to a distance from the center according to the length of time the meeting was expected to last.

The assembly took their seats in order. The outer end of the spiral circle was set afire, and immediately rose into a bright flame which slowly and gradually crept round the central pillar, affording a gentle and sufficient light. Two warriors then entered together at the door, each bearing large conch shells full of the black drink. They advanced with slow and uniform steps, their faces uplifted. Coming within a few paces of the seats of the Beloved Man and the white leaders, they stopped together. Each rested his shell on a little table, then took it up again and, bowing low, presented it.

As soon as the shell was raised to the mouth a servant uttered two notes which continued as long as he had breath. As long as these notes continued, so long must the person drink. These notes were very solemn and struck the imagination with a religious awe.

The whole assembly was treated in this manner, as long as the drink and the light continued to hold out. Simultaneous with the drinking, pipes were brought. A skin of panther, stuffed with tobacco, was laid before the Beloved Man's feet, together with a beautifully adorned great or royal pipe. Skins of tobacco were likewise cast at the feet of the first white man and from him passed to others to fill their pipes.

The Beloved Man smoked the great pipe first, blowing the first few whiffs off ceremoniously towards the Great Spirit, next towards the four cardinal points, then towards the white people present. The great pipe was taken from the Creek chief by a servant and presented to the chief white man, Lincoln, from whom it circulated round the assemblage in the order of their standing and importance.

Lincoln and Griffin managed to get through the ceremony without becoming ill, but David Humphreys was less fortunate. The combination of black drink and tobacco smoke in the crowded tent made him first pale, then green, and finally he put his plump white hand to his mouth and rushed outside. The Creeks could not hide their smiles at this weakness of a man who was reputed to be a great warrior. Humphreys

was later to charge that McGillivray had deliberately humiliated him by seeing to it that he drank more than his share
of "that vile black stuff that tasted like nothing more than a
puree of frogs, mud and rotten whiskey."

The next day the treaty talks, which Alexander McGillivray insisted be conducted and concluded in the Indian
camp, were opened. General Lincoln spoke, or in the words
of the Creeks, "gave out his talk," and then put a draft copy
of the treaty in McGillivray's hands, to be considered at his
leisure. Colonel Humphreys followed Lincoln with a general
speech full of overinflated phrases such as "red brothers" and
"eternal peace," not neglecting to annoy the chiefs by including a panegyric to the power and strength of the United
States which had "warriors as the blades of grass and which
had conquered all their enemies."

That evening the Beloved Man assembled the chiefs in his
tent and explained the treaty to them, making particular
objection to two articles. One article stated that the Creek
acknowledged themselves to be under the protection of the
United States and of no other sovereign, and also that they
were not to hold any treaty with any other state. The other
article, relating to the boundary dispute with Georgia, not
only confirmed all the Oconee lands to the state, but went
further to include all the island and streams of the St. Mary's
River, branches of which extended to both the waters of
the St. John's River in East Florida and to the Okafinoka
swamps in Seminole country.

The Beloved Man summed up his reaction to the commissioners' demands by commenting: "We are told that
President Washington was going to limit the Georgian
demands in the interests of justice. The thieving Georgians
must have had his ears and his eyes both, for he has not only
gone along with them but attempted to intimidate us by
asking for three times as much as what the Georgians were
initially demanding."

One of the chiefs moved that the Creeks respond to this

insult by breaking camp and returning to the Nation without notification to the Americans. Alexander shook his head. "This is exactly what the Georgians want, to accuse us in their legislature and in their newspapers of leaving before replying to their demands, and thus breaking faith. No, we must play the farce out to its curtain."

In the morning Alexander sent the commissioners a letter flatly rejecting the two articles in question. Upon receipt of it, Colonel Humphreys came over to argue him out of his objections. When he saw that both flattery and intimidation were useless, he tried bribery. If Colonel McGillivray would agree to the American terms his father's estates would be restored to him in full.

"My dear Colonel," Alex replied, "you Americans made me a poor man. Through my own efforts I have now become fairly comfortable. Do you think I would become a rich man at the price of my integrity and that of my people?"

"You misunderstand," said Humphreys. "We did not intend this offer as a bribe. We regard it as a just property restitution."

"If that is the case then surely you will restore my father's property and estates whether or not I sign the treaty."

"I did not say that," muttered Humphreys confusedly, thrown for a loss. "Such a restitution would have to be worked out with the Georgia authorities, who resist it." This, thought Alex contemptuously, was the American statesman who had represented his country to such applause in London and Paris. The meeting ended soon thereafter, after Alex had refused various valuable gifts sent to him by Washington.

The next day General Lincoln invited Alex to the American camp for discussions, but the latter demurred. Finally the three commissioners showed up in a body, to restate their demands and offer gifts to the Creek chiefs in Alexander's presence. Although it was difficult for an Indian to conceive why he should reject any present whatsoever, a fact passed along to the commissioners by their Georgian advisers, the chiefs unanimously refused the presents. Only Cyrus Griffin had the good grace to be embarrassed at this flagrant attempt to compromise Alexander McGillivray's authority with his chiefs and headmen.

General Lincoln broke the impasse by saying that there was a possibility that the St. Mary's demands could be adjusted.

"Even if they were eliminated entirely we would still be faced with the loss of our Oconee lands, and absolutely no protection except from the nation which has seen fit to collaborate with our enemies, the Georgians. My answer, gentlemen, is no."

"Colonel McGillivray, you are damnably uncooperative!" Humphreys shot at him.

Alex smiled. "To say the least, Colonel."

After the meeting Alexander told his chiefs that there was no point in further wrangling, and that the Creeks should retreat as peaceably as they had come. The following day the Creek camp was struck. Alex and his party had gone as far as the Okmulgee River when he was overtaken by General Pickens, who urged him to return to Rock Landing.

"I will pledge myself that the commissioners will consent to treat with you on equal terms," said Pickens.

"Does this mean that the commissioners agree to make restitution of the Oconee lands?"

"I cannot promise that," said the American.

"In that case, General," said Alexander, "I can only continue on," and signaled his party to move forward.

Yet on reflection Alex decided that the conference had not been a complete fiasco; during it he had been able to talk with a number of American officers who had asked him his opinion of moving westward. He had encouraged them; it was better to have such men, among the most troublesome neighbors of the Creek, behind them rather than in their

General Andrew Pickens

way. Several had shamelessly agreed to correspond with and give him information of what went on in their country. There were, they said, at least fifteen hundred families in Georgia who were awaiting developments between the Creeks and the Georgians before moving over the frontier.

The disgruntled commissioners returned to New York to report to President Washington. Alex, after himself reporting to Governor Miró, received word from him expressing his anxiety that the commissioners would misrepresent Alex's intentions and persuade Washington and the Congress that he had merely seized a pretext to continue hostilities. He urged that Alexander avoid putting obstacles in the way of renewed negotiations next spring. However, Miró added that he had given orders for delivery to the Creeks of 785 guns, via William Panton's pack trains. (About which Louis Milfort commented appositely: "The Spaniards want to eat their tortillas and have them, too!")

These guns were at least partly the result of an intercession on the part of William Panton, under heavy obligation to Alexander McGillivray. Panton now had large trading establishments at all the important posts of Florida. At his chief store in Pensacola he employed fifteen clerks. Here also was the Panton and Leslie "skin house," where the valuable skins and rich furs were packed for foreign markets. He employed no less than fifteen schooners.

Now when Alexander McGillivray asked for a favor, William Panton hastened to oblige him. The Scot could not afford to alienate the man who had made him, as Lachlan McGillivray had once predicted he would become, the first millionaire merchant prince of America.

Under a charter of Charles II, Georgia claimed all the territory from the Savannah to the Mississippi, lying between 31° and 35°. In 1785 she had established the county of Bourbon, embracing the settlements along the Mississippi above and below Natchez, but Spanish occupation had prevented its settlement.

In 1789 the Georgia General Assembly authorized a sale of the larger portion of this wild country. For a little more than $60,000, five million acres were sold to the South Carolina Yazoo Company. Seven million acres were sold to the Virginia Yazoo Company for around $93,000, and three million five thousand acres in northern Alabama went to the Tennessee Yazoo Company for $46,000.

Spain claimed much of this territory by conquests made towards the close of the Revolutionary War. Spain and the United States were now negotiating to settle the boundaries, but Georgia proceeded to take the matter into her own hands.

Alarmed by the potential collision that he anticipated be-

tween the United States government, Georgia, Spain and the
Indians as a result of this extraordinary sale of territory,
President Washington issued a proclamation against the entire enterprise. The Tennessee Company ignored the federal edict. Zacha-
riah Coxe, its head, made his way by flatboat to Muscle
Shoals. Here he built a blockhouse intended to back up his
sale of much of the best land north and south of the Tennessee River. But the Cherokees, incited by Governor Blount
of Tennessee, who was an active agent of Washington, attacked Coxe at Muscle Shoals and expelled him from the
country.

Washington was as ruthless with the representative of the
South Carolina Yazoo Company, James O'Fallon, who went
to Kentucky and raised troops with the intention of taking
the Natchez country from the Spaniards and selling it to
settlers. The President had O'Fallon arrested and ordered
General St. Clair to put down by military force all attempts
to colonize the Natchez country. Alexander McGillivray was
not uninvolved in these proceedings; the speculators knew
that his name on the board of directors of a land company
would serve as a guarantee against Indian attacks, and would
do much to stimulate land sales. He was offered huge sums
for his cooperation, but in every instance rejected them,
replying that the lands in question were owned by either
Spain or the Indians. The Tennessee Company grant included every foot of the Cherokee, Chickasaw and Creek
hunting grounds.

The first Yazoo speculations, which ended in disaster for
their backers, were indirectly responsible for the journey of
Colonel Marinus Willett to the Creek Nation, which resulted in the signing of the New York Treaty between the
Creeks and the United States.

George Washington's first impulse, after the return of
Lincoln, Humphreys and Griffin to New York, was to invade
the Creeks and force them to relinquish the Oconee lands.

He was influenced in this course, against his better judgment, by the pressure of the Georgia Congressional delegation. But when Washington learned that the expense of such a war would amount to fifteen million dollars, a sum the new nation could ill afford, he abandoned the idea of a war. The difficulties, he believed, could yet be settled by negotiation in person between himself and Alexander McGillivray.

To this end he selected Marinus Willett, an officer who had distinguished himself in the Revolution, to visit the Creek Nation as a secret agent and try to return with McGillivray to New York. Willett was ordered to keep his mission a secret from all except General Pickens.

Willett sailed from New York with a servant and two horses, and arrived in Charleston after a passage of fourteen days. In mid-April, 1790, he reached the home of General Pickens on the Seneca River.

Pickens provided Willett with an Indian guide for the Cherokee country, and he set out to complete his lonely mission. Passing through Cherokee country, Willett reached Eustanee, a town similar to those of the Creeks, where bloodshed was forbidden. Here he witnessed an Indian ball game, for him a novel and exciting experience.

On April 28 Colonel Willett proceeded to the Creek Nation, and stopped at the home of a Mr. Scott, a trader of the Creeks. Learning from Scott that Alexander McGillivray was at the moment on a visit to Oakfuskee, on the Tallapoosa River, Willett decided to meet him at the Creek town. He arrived only a few hours before Alexander was scheduled to leave for Little Tallassie, and immediately delivered Washington's letter to him.

In his letter Washington invited the Indian chief to New York, where he wished to sign with him a treaty of peace and alliance. The United States, he said, wanted none of the Creek land. The President was ready to promote and facilitate trade by enabling the Creeks to procure goods in a cheap and easy manner. He also stood ready to guarantee other measures that would contribute to the welfare and happiness of the Creek Nation.

Alexander and the envoy from New York took an immediate liking to one another. On his part, Willett, as he was later to write in the narrative of his journey, found the Creek chief a "man of open and generous mind, with an excellent judgment and a very tenacious memory." On Alexander's part, Willett recommended himself on several grounds.

First, the Long Islander bore a personal letter from the greatest American of his day, a man for whom Alexander had tremendous admiration, and on whom he modeled himself as the Washington of the Creek Nation. Secondly Willett was friendly, unassuming and intelligent. He had no preconceived notion about the justice of the American point of view, and was frank enough to say so. He quite delighted Alexander by telling him that Washington had considered a war against the Creeks and then abandoned it because of the national pocketbook. Lincoln's report, he added, had not only misrepresented Alexander McGillivray as a man with whom it was impossible to reach an agreement, but had included suggestions for the establishment of a chain of American forts in Creek country.

Willett was honored by a dance in the Hillabee town, and observed the ceremony of the black drink. Then he and the Beloved Man left for Little Tallassie. Immediately upon their arrival there, Alexander sent word to the Creek chiefs to meet at Ositchy, in ten days, for a conference to be addressed by Willett.

After reflection on Washington's letter he had decided to go to New York. He had one main reason, and this was neither Washington's invitation nor Marinus Willett's charm. Spain and England might well be going to war over the Nootka issue, which had arisen from conflicting British and Spanish claims to the northwest coast of North America. If war came, Panton's trade would be seriously affected and

Spain might find it impossible to supply the Creeks with arms and ammunition. In addition, Washington had hinted, and Willett had borne him out, that the United States government was reluctant to go to war with the Creeks not only because of the expense involved but because Georgia would reap all and the government none of the advantages if such a conflict were brought to a successful conclusion. The national government, to put it bluntly, did not want Georgia to have title to the western lands included in the Yazoo grants; it wanted title for itself. To this end President Washington, Willett said, was willing to concede unusually favorable terms to the Creeks, terms that would not conflict with those they had already arranged with the Spaniards. Finally, the Yazoo speculators were proving at least initially successful with the Chickasaws, who were ceding them large tracts of land. Under the circumstances a rupture between the Chickasaw and the Creek was probable, and the Creek would have the help of a national government in any warfare with their neighbors. They would get none from the Spaniards, whose policy it was to cultivate both tribes.

"The Spaniards will be less than enthusiastic," Louis Milfort commented when Alex briefed him on his decision.

"Why should they object?" asked Alex, grinning. "Haven't the Spaniards always urged me to make peace with the Americans?"

"But they never really expected you would, at least not in New York, where Washington will be able to press for his advantage. Now they'll try to stop you."

"It's too late," said Alexander.

William Panton, who did not want Alexander McGillivray to make peace with the Americans, rushed three hundred miles from Chickasaw country to stop him, but he arrived a day too late. On May 12 McGillivray and Washington's envoy had set off into the wilderness for New York.

X

THE TREATY OF
NEW YORK

The entourage arrived at the town of Tuckabatchee at
five o'clock, and spent the evening there. The next day it
crossed the Tallapoosa River, and reached Coweta, on the
Chattahoochie. It arrived at Ositchy the next morning, and
awaited the chiefs of the Creek Confederacy whom Alexander had called to the conference.

Colonel Willett addressed the assembly that morning. He
said he had been sent a far distance by his great chief,
George Washington, to invite the chiefs to his council house
in New York. Here Washington wished to sign with Alexander McGillivray a treaty of peace and alliance in which
their territory and trade would be secured. This treaty would
be "as strong as the hills and lasting as the rivers."

Then the Hollowing King, a prominent Creek orator,
rose to speak.

"We are glad to see you," he addressed Willett. "You have
come a great way, and as soon as we fixed our eyes upon you
we were made glad. We are poor, and have not the knowledge of the white people except for our beloved man, Alexander McGillivray. We were invited to the treaty at Rock
Landing. Nothing was done, and we returned from it with
sorrow. The road to your great council house is long, and
the weather is hot; but our beloved chief shall go with you,
and such others as we may appoint. We will agree to all
things which our beloved chief shall do. We will count the
time he is away, and when he comes back we shall be glad
to see him bearing from the Watcina a treaty 'as strong as the

hills and lasting as the rivers.' May you be preserved from every evil!"

Two days later the entourage, swelled by the addition of a dozen chiefs, arrived at Coweta where Willett partook of the black drink and received a speech from the White Lieutenant of the Upper Creeks. On the following day the group arrived back at Little Tallassie. Here Willett sent a letter to Henry Knox, the Secretary of War.

The party set out for New York, mounted on horseback and accompanied by several pack horses. Taking a north-easterly direction through the wilderness, it arrived at Stone Mountain, Georgia, on June 1, where it was joined by the Coweta and Cussitah chiefs.

The party reached the home of General Pickens at Seneca where it received a warm welcome, and was joined by Chinobe, the great Natchez warrior, and other chiefs. When the expedition set out again it contained three wagons in which twenty-six chiefs and warriors rode. Alexander and his suite were on horseback, and Willett rode in a sulky.

At Guildford Court House, in North Carolina, there was an affecting scene. Some years before the Creeks had killed a man named Brown and kidnapped his wife and children whom they brought to Little Tallassie. As he had done on similar occasions, Alexander paid their ransoms and maintained the woman and her children at his plantation for over a year. Mrs. Brown and her family had later returned to her home state.

Hearing of the colonel's arrival, Mrs. Brown rushed through the crowd and almost overpowered her benefactor with protestations of her admiration for him and her gratitude for his having saved their lives.

In both Richmond and Fredericksburg, Alexander McGillivray and his party were received by prominent citizens. At Philadelphia the festivities continued for three days.

Philadelphia was the largest town in the United States,

and yet it seemed no more than a big village. The houses, though attractive with their red brick, white trim and polished brass, had no numbers. There were no postmen; as in Charleston, a citizen who wanted to mail a letter had to carry it to the post office, where he also called for his mail. Of course there was little letter writing. Ordinary people who were not in business sometimes passed a year or two without receiving a letter of any kind.

Yet Philadelphia far surpassed cities like Charleston and New Orleans in civic improvements. Public street lights had been in effect for some time. There were no vultures, who served as natural scavengers, in the streets. Dan McGillivray, Alex's young nephew, marveled at the Philadelphia fire department, consisting of volunteer firemen organized into companies. Yet Alexander observed that the fire department, while impressive, was not very effective. It depended on pumps in the yards and in the streets, and usually a burning house burned down before the firemen arrived.

A love of bright colors seemed more prevalent in Philadelphia than in any city Alexander had seen. The women were brilliant in silks, velvets and brocades. There were many foppish men to be seen in the streets carrying gold snuffboxes and gold-headed canes. This atmosphere of luxury—Pennsylvania was the most prosperous of the states—extended to the table. At the home of a rich merchant to which Marinus Willett and Alexander were invited for dinner, the guests consumed turtle, fowl and pork; flummery, jellies and sweetmeats; trifles, whipped syllabubs and floating island, and desserts of fruits, raisins, almonds, peaches and pears.

The party boarded a sloop at Elizabethtown Point and landed in New York. It was met at Murray's Wharf by a military escort and the largest crowd that had assembled since Washington's inauguration fifteen months before. The Tammany Society, in full Indian regalia, made a more gorgeous sight than did the real Indian warriors after their long and arduous journey.

The cavalcade was marched up Wall Street to Federal Hall, where Congress was then in session, and next to the house of the President, to whom they were introduced with much pomp and ceremony.

Alexander found Washington cordial, although it was hard for so glacially dignified a man to be warm and unofficial. But he felt they had taken one another's measure, liked what they saw, and had a basic mutual understanding.

"I am glad you have come, Colonel," the President said simply in greeting. "I have long felt we had much in common."

"I cannot flatter myself that much, Mr. President," Alexander replied, "but it has long been my ambition to shake your hand in friendship."

Many years later historians, bearing out what George Washington said on the occasion, were to write that here, on the stoop of the President's house, on July 17, 1790, were brought face to face the most remarkable white and red men the Western Hemisphere had yet produced.

The delegation then visited Secretary of War Knox, and Governor De Witt Clinton. A sumptuous entertainment at the City Tavern concluded the day. Alex and young Dan McGillivray returned with their host, Henry Knox, to the latter's residence. The other chiefs camped about a mile from town.

In the next days Washington's strategy became clear. He had decided that since the Creek chief had rejected all formal overtures in the past, present negotiations should be conducted informally between Henry Knox and McGillivray. In the event of an impasse Washington would lend his immense prestige to the American side.

Knox had not shown much understanding of Creek problems in his recommendations to Washington for the Lincoln-

Humphreys-Griffin mission. Nor did he show much now. Thus Washington was constantly called in to arbitrate their discussions and disagreements. The President was a shrewd negotiator, with a mind that worked much faster than that of any other American with whom Alexander had dealt.

On the third day of talks Alex received a letter from Carlos Howard, Spanish chargé d'affaires at St. Augustine. Howard had been sent on "sick leave" to, of all places, Philadelphia. It was plain why he was there; to prevent, if possible, the signing of an American treaty by Alexander.

Spain, Howard wrote, was the only natural ally and protector of the southern Indian. Along with granting them a tariff-free trade, she had not and never would ask for an inch of their territory.

The Americans, Howard went on, obviously had different intentions. For the present the United States might concede the lands under disputation, but in future, when the Creeks had broken their ties with Spain, "not only the disputed lands but also the last foot of Creek territory will be gradually usurped, until you will cease to be a nation. Turn your eyes to the north; reflect on what those tribes were in past times, and realize what they are today. The English and French were in truth the first usurpers, but the Americans have already begun to imitate them, and will continue to do so until they have reduced the Creeks to the same level on which are now those who were once so powerful, their now almost annihilated brothers."

The Spaniard insisted that the Crown had no objection to a permanent peace between the Creeks and the United States. "My sovereign is on friendly terms with the United States, and if they have as honest intentions as does Spain, they will not attempt or even desire through a treaty to destroy the connections that have existed for a long time between the Creek Nation and the Spaniards."

Did Colonel McGillivray, continued Howard, have any

propositions to make to the court at Madrid? If so, these could be transmitted through Baron Don Josef Ignacio de Viar, a Spanish official currently in New York. If so, the colonel might also communicate to De Viar "all the questions that may be treated by you and the Congress or its commissioners." * Howard did not doubt that De Viar would be in touch with the Colonel, "difficult as this might be, considering the jealous watch the Americans must be keeping over you."

This was nothing more than a last-minute attempt at bribery; the Spaniards were trying to avoid a Creek-American treaty by buying him off.

The very next day, Don Josef called at Knox's residence. The Spaniard glanced nervously about Knox's parlor and said, "Perhaps, Colonel, we could talk more comfortably at my own quarters?"

"You must realize, Don Josef, that I am a guest of Secretary Knox's. When I leave his house a military escort accompanies me wherever I go."

"How clever of the Americans to chaperone you so carefully," De Viar commented drily. "Have you had an opportunity to read Howard's letter?"

"Baron, Spain desires that I conclude peace with the Americans, respecting at all times our treaty with Spain. This I intend to do. My refusal of the American propositions at Rock Landing last September came near to causing very serious consequences. In spite of the fact that the attitude of the Georgians towards us is generally condemned, my hasty refusal was considered as an insult to the dignity of the United States. Had I not come to New York, Congress would have undoubtedly declared war on us, and we have no solid basis for supposing or hoping that Spain would go to war to sustain our claims."

* From *McGillivray of the Creeks,* by John Walton Caughey. Copyright 1938 by the University of Oklahoma Press.

"The United States is in no position to begin a war," said De Viar.

"My dear Baron, that is a matter of opinion."

De Viar changed his tack. "Washington will insist on American sovereignty over the Creek Nation, not only on those parts of your nation that are within the United States."

"It is one thing to insist, Don Josef, another to get."

"Spain would be much disturbed at such an arrangement, violating as it would the Pensacola Treaty of 1784."

"There will be no violations of the treaty."

"We believe that Washington will try to set your boundaries far west, in order to pacify the Georgians. Are you prepared to sacrifice your western lands?"

"The negotiations have just begun."

"Washington and Knox," persisted the Spaniard, "will strive hard to get an American trade."

"I am loyal to William Panton. I would consent to an emergency trade only in case war between Spain and England closed existing channels. Tell me, Baron, would you say war between England and Spain was impossible?"

De Viar was forced to admit that he could not say so. "In any case, you will keep us informed of the negotiations as they progress?"

Alexander smiled. "When your representatives are negotiating with the United States on the disputed boundary, can I expect you to keep me informed of your conversations?"

The Spaniard didn't attempt to answer this question. He said, "Colonel, we are prepared to offer you a secret commission as brigadier general with a salary of two thousand dollars a year, if only you will brief us on your more significant conversations with the Americans as they occur."

Alex refused categorically and a short time later De Viar departed. One of Knox's aides, sitting in the hall, saw him to his carriage.

Not only the Spanish, but the British attempted to get

Alexander McGillivray's ear during his negotiations with Washington and Knox. Major George Beckwith requested an interview to ask whether William Augustus Bowles, now at Quebec with a handful of Indians, was an authorized representative of the southern Indians, as he claimed.

Alexander laughed. "Is that scoundrel up to his plots and strategems again? No, Major, I can tell you that Bowles represents only his employers and himself. And that none too skillfully."

He was underestimating the Maryland adventurer. Bowles was soon to cause him more trouble than he could have believed possible.

Beckwith tried to pump him for information on the negotiations in New York, but Alexander refused to oblige. "The English abandoned the Creeks and their trade," he told him. "They also rescinded my commission. You can understand why I do not feel their interests are any longer those of my people."

The Americans could not stop the Spanish and British visits, but they discouraged them as much as they could. When Baron de Viar reappeared for another interview, he was told Colonel McGillivray was in conference with the President, when the truth was that he was taking a nap. A messenger for Beckwith, bearing a thank-you note for the interview with Alexander and asking for another, was turned rudely away. Alexander noticed that he was being followed to and from the Indian camp.

The negotiations had begun to fatigue him, and splitting headaches were becoming more and more frequent as the nervous strain told. He missed his wife and children and wished he had brought Louis Milfort along as a confidant; he badly needed a man of subtle mind who spoke his own language. Washington was being advised by men of the brilliance and caliber of Thomas Jefferson and Alexander Hamilton; he had no one. The Spanish were suspicious of him.

Although Secretary Knox had conceived a genuine fondness for Dan McGillivray and talked about adopting him, and Alex could not have wished for better hospitality at the Americans' tables, they were, after all, his antagonists in a trading match that might decide the future of his Nation.

Washington was taking an increasing part in the negotiations, and Alexander felt hard pressed to hold his own. The President was used to command and did not care to be disputed; challenge him on a matter of fact and his glacial reserve became even more marked. Although Alexander had successfully argued against an acknowledgment of American sovereignty, except over the part of the Creek Nation that lay within United States limits, the effect of this provision was to make ultimate Creek boundaries dependent upon the settlement of the disputed boundary between the United States and Spain. If, after the boundary settlement, all or part of the Creek territory should lie north or east of the ultimate line, it would be under American protection. Any part south or west of the line would be under protection of the Spanish Crown.

Washington had also scored to his advantage on the issue of the boundary between the Creeks and the United States. He was adamant on the Oconee lands, insisting that the Georgians could not be expelled from the territories on which they had already settled because it would take additional bloodshed to remove them. To his own advantage, Alexander managed to get the boundary set less far west than Georgia demanded, and the Creeks gained a valuable hunting area on the Altahama River. Financial compensation for surrender of the Oconee lands was set at ten thousand dollars in merchandise and an annual payment to the Creek Nation of two thousand dollars.

Knox pounded without letup on the authorization of an American trade, but Alexander would not compromise his loyalty to Panton. He would consent only to an arrangement for an emergency trade should war between England and Spain close existing trade channels. In this case fifty thousand dollars' worth of goods annually might be imported duty free from the United States into the Creek country. This provision was part of a secret article which also provided that the question of American trade might be brought up again after two years. Another secret article provided that the Americans feed, clothe and educate, in the north, at their own expense, up to four Creek youths at a time.

In addition, also under another secret article, Alexander was to receive a commission as a brigadier general in the army of the United States at a salary of $1,800 a year. This was in compensation for the losses of his father's estate until the state of Georgia could be prevailed upon to restore these losses in full.

There were several other provisions: all traders without a license from the United States government were to be excluded from the Creek towns; the Creeks were authorized to expel by force any intruders on the lands guaranteed to them by the treaty, thus sounding the death knell of the Yazoo companies; white persons and Negroes captured by the Creeks during the recent hostilities were to be returned at Rock Landing; the leading Creek chiefs were to receive from the United States an annual pension of one hundred dollars.

On August 17, 1790 the treaty of peace and friendship between the United States and the Creek Nation was solemnly ratified by the contracting parties at Federal Hall. A correspondent of the *Pennsylvania Packet and Daily Advertiser* described the ceremony: "At 12 o'clock the President of the United States and his suite—General Knox, the Commissioner; the clerks of the department of the Secretary of War; Colonel McGillivray, and the kings, chiefs and warriors of the Creek Nation being assembled, the treaty was read by the President's secretary.

"The President then addressed the assemblage. He said that he thought the treaty just and equal, and stated the mutual duties of the contracting parties, which address was communicated sentence after sentence by the interpreter, to all of which the Creeks gave an audible assent.

"The President then signed the treaty, after which he presented to Colonel McGillivray several books and one of the epaulettes of his uniform, worn during the late war, and to the chiefs a string of beads of perpetual peace and a paper of tobacco to smoke in remembrance. Mr. McGillivray rose, made a short reply to the President, and received the tokens.

"This was succeeded by the shake of peace, every one of the Creeks passing this friendly salute with the President. A song of peace, performed by the Creeks, concluded this highly interesting, solemn and dignified transaction."

The *Packet*'s correspondent was also on hand for the dinner held two days later by the St. Andrews Society at the City Tavern in the colonel's honor. "The Society," he wrote, "anxious to show their respect to Colonel McGillivray, unanimously elected him an honorary member of the Society . . . The Colonel was introduced to the presiding figures, and received the compliments of the Society. Later he partook of a collation provided for the occasion, and mingled with great affability in the festivity of the evening . . ." *

Next day the Creek delegation sailed to the St. Mary's River on their journey homeward. Accompanying them, as deputy Indian agent, was a young army lieutenant, Caleb Swan. It was Swan's intention to observe the Creek's customs, manners and ceremonies in order to record them for posterity.

In general Alexander was satisfied by the Treaty of New

* From *McGillivray of the Creeks,* by John Walton Caughey. Copyright 1938 by the University of Oklahoma Press.

York. He had not yielded to the United States on anything it had not already taken; or anything the Creeks, by contesting, could hope to hold against the power of the American nation. He knew it would be said by his critics that he had surrendered the Oconee country for an inadequate payment. The obvious answer to this was that he had exhausted every expedient his fertile mind could command to stay Georgia's encroachments without a war that would destroy his people. In addition, he now had the plighted faith of the United States, in the person of George Washington, that no further encroachments would be made.

His critics would also charge that he had gained personal advantages at the conference table at the expense of his people. This was unfair. The Creeks felt that to honor him was to honor them, and the power of the Nation. Not a single chief had expressed disapproval of his commission as a brigadier.

His ultimate justification would be this: in time, the eventual charge of the British, the Spanish and the Americans that they had failed to make him their dupe. What could be better proof of his fidelity to his people?

Caleb Swan joined him at the rail of the schooner. "I'm glad to see you taking the sea breeze, Colonel," the young officer said. "You have been looking fatigued."

"Yes, Lieutenant. It's been a long trip. Six weeks' travel to New York, and a month there, during which I had to take to my bed several times with these infernal sick headaches. And now the return voyage. I'll be glad to get home."

The shade of the apple orchard, the serenity of the Coosa under its willows and cypress, the peace of his study with its books and manuscripts beckoned him invitingly. He would be satisfied never to leave Little Tallassie again.

XI

THE ALIEN SANDS

On his return home Alexander learned that in his absence Sophia Durant had been at the center of a drama that was still being discussed by the people of the area.

Sophia's air of authority had increased with the years, and together with her beauty it had made her quite a formidable person. Much more familiar with the Creek language than her brother, on many occasions when he had held Councils in the vicinity of Little Tallassie she had delivered his speeches for him.

In August, while Alexander was in New York, the Creeks of a nearby town had risen against a white settlement. Although she was pregnant with her third child, Sophia, with characteristic McGillivray boldness, had mounted a horse and, acompanied only by her Negro maid, ridden three days to the town that had taken the warpath. There she had assembled the chiefs and, holding over them the vengeance of her brother, forced them to call back their war party. Only a week later the remarkable Sophia gave birth to twin boys.

As Alex had anticipated, the Georgians were not long in attacking the Treaty of New York as a betrayal of their state. In Congress Representative James Jackson charged that the treaty had "given away three million acres of land guaranteed to Georgia by the Constitution" and had "contemptuously disregarded" the commissioners' report of 1789. He also complained that the treaty had contained secret articles that could only be to the disadvantage of Georgia. The government, Jackson said, had given away Georgia's land, invited a savage to its seat of government, "caressed him in a most extraordinary manner, and sent him home loaded with favors."

An organization was formed in Georgia called the Combined Society of Friends, whose avowed purpose was to drive the Creeks from those lands its members considered to be the property of the state.

Nor were the Spaniards, or William Panton, pleased by the Treaty of New York. Alexander's concessions to the Americans, they said, were excessive; he had responded too much to American flattery. He had sworn allegiance to the United States; did not this invalidate his allegiance to Spain? His commission as a brigadier in the United States army, and the annual salary that went with it, they interpreted not as partial restitution for the loss of Lachlan McGillivray's estates but as another indication of his being bound to the American interest. They objected to Knox's adoption of Dan McGillivray as the first Creek youth to be educated in the states as showing a predilection for the Americans. They even suspected that Caleb Swan had come to the Creek Nation to destroy the Indians' attachment to Spain.

Yet these criticisms of Howard, O'Neill and Miró, forwarded to the Spanish court, had an effect opposite from what was intended. The court urged that the Indian chief's friendship be cultivated even more intensively, now that he showed signs of defection. His pension was increased to two thousand pesos a year. An additional reason for this generosity may have been the recent rumor that General George Rogers Clark of Kentucky was secretly preparing a force to attack the Spanish posts on the Mississippi. In such an event the Spaniards wanted to be able to count on the friendship of the southern Indians.

In the winter of 1791 Alexander McGillivray had reached the height of his career. President Washington had recognized him as the head of his Nation, and the United States government was pledged to guarantee Creek territory against encroachments by Georgia, the land companies and Cumberland. The Spaniards, though mistrustful of him, were courting his favor more eagerly than ever. His family life was idyllic. Had it not been for new bouts with rheumatism and sick headaches, his cup would have runneth over.

He and Caleb Swan had become good friends. Swan came to him with his manuscript on Creek manners and customs, and Alexander advised him on questions relating to it. He was invaluable to the American in clearing up certain misconceptions.

For example, Swan found it difficult to account for the Creeks' dignified deportment and bearing, which set them off from their Indian neighbors. Alex explained it in this way: "Since the Creeks' frontier is open to their enemies on all sides, they find themselves under the necessity of banding together in large towns. These towns are close together, as is necessary to defend themselves in case of sudden invasion. This consequently makes deer and bear scarce, which in turn obliges the Creek to be vigilant and industrious. And these qualities naturally beget care and serious attention, which we may suppose in some degree form their natural disposition towards gravity of bearing."

Swan was equally struck by the Creek custom of keeping the white man's Sabbath. On Sundays Little Tallassie was silent and solemn; if a child chanced to stray outside he was quickly drawn indoors again. Alex explained that the Creek kept the Sabbath merely out of respect to the white men in their midst, even though there might be only one present. He observed ruefully that he wished the white man, over his long association with the Creek, had shown him equal respect and consideration.

The lieutenant was often present on those occasions when the Beloved Man presided over altercations and disputes.

Swan noticed that Alexander rarely handed down a decision, and asked why. "Because," said Alexander, "a decision against one of the parties involved would end in bad feeling on the part of the other. This way the matter usually works its way out, or is eventually forgotten."

But if the lieutenant thought Alexander McGillivray held a loose rein over his people he was mistaken. The Beloved Man had instituted a number of radical reforms, including replacement of the Micos, the hereditary kings, by the warrior chiefs of the Creek towns; the ending of the barbarous Creek custom of killing the slaves of a deceased master; severe penalization of horse thieves, and the forbidding of overindulgence in spiritous liquors. Although successfully brought about, none of these changes had been easy to carry out, and often he had been obliged to use strong measures.

Swan was shocked by the Creek custom of rewarding a successful physician with generous payments in skins and cattle, and penalizing that physician who failed his patient with severe beatings and even death. "This should demonstrate," Alex said, "how firmly the Creek is wedded to superstition. If a patient dies the doctor is considered a witch or sorcerer, influenced by the devil, and he is treated accordingly. This has one good effect; there are not many among the Creek who take up the medical profession!"

In late 1791 Alexander McGillivray's hard-won calm was rudely shattered by the reappearance of William Augustus Bowles in the Creek Nation.

On his last departure, engineered by the Spaniards in 1789, Bowles had persuaded a few Creeks and Cherokee half-breeds to accompany him to the Bahamas. Once there he had betrayed half of his followers by selling them to slave dealers. Within a short time he was in jail for debt, but with the help of Lord Dunmore managed to escape to the Florida Keys. There the Florida Indians would have killed him and his men had not chance put the adventurer in the way of a wrecked Spanish schooner that had valuable cargo aboard.

Bowles had bought off the hostile Indians, dressed his followers in impressive uniforms found in the Spanish ship, and hired a passing fishing boat to sail him and his men to Halifax, Nova Scotia. There he had introduced himself to the governor as a man of consequence, and his followers as important chiefs. Bowles had been so convincing that the governor sent him on to Lord Dorchester, governor general of Canada, who paid his passage to London.

London swallowed whole the adventurer and his entourage. Bowles dined with cabinet ministers and was entertained by prominent personages; he was passed on to the Spanish ambassador as a man of the greatest importance among the southern Indians.

With English funds he returned to Nassau in the summer of 1791, where he renewed his alliance with Governor Dunmore and Miller and persuaded both to sponsor his new enterprise to supplant Alexander McGillivray as "Emperor of the Creeks" and William Panton as trader to the Creek Nation. Notwithstanding that Miller had already spent two thousand pounds in backing his earlier failure, the merchant advanced the adventurer another thousand.

Bowles returned to Creek country from the Bahamas in September. Not long after reports came to Alexander that "Captain Liar," as the Lower Creeks called him, was telling the Indians that he had come to save them from McGillivray, who had sold their lands to the Americans. The adventurer showed a commission from the British Secretary of State appointing him "Superintendent General of the Creek Nation," and he had also brought a flag and a great seal.

"Bowles has now added forgery to his arsenal of weapons," Milfort said. "You should have listened to me and got rid of him in '89."

"We will pay a visit to Captain Liar," said Alex.

But it was not so easy to see the freebooter. Bowles's father-in-law said he was not at home, and though Alex knew otherwise, he could not make the chief a liar by calling on Bowles and finding him in hiding. Nor could he seize him; Creek custom forbade violence in a friend's town.

Before returning to Tallassie he visited Bowles's warehouse and was gratified to find that the trade goods Bowles had brought were scanty, hardly enough to even challenge Panton's ascendency. Bowles's influence among the Indians could not last very long.

Yet in the next few months Alex had to admit that he was wrong. Bowles's charm and personality were such that he was moving successfully to solidify his position. A large number of restless Lower Creek warriors had joined him, eager to follow a man who, unlike Alexander McGillivray, held out the promise of plunder. His supporters had recognized him as the "Director of Affairs" of the Creek Nation. In their name he wrote Governor O'Neill, announcing his friendship for Spain, offering a Creek and Cherokee alliance, and demanding navigation privileges. Shrewdly he played on old Spanish suspicions of Alexander McGillivray to charge that the Beloved Man was actively soliciting the friendship of the United States.

The Spaniards were upset enough by Bowles's claim of Creek support to ask Panton if he considered Bowles an active threat to McGillivray's authority, in which case they would have to reckon with him. Panton replied that Bowles was a vagabond and mountebank whose dubious influence would soon fade. But he was cautious enough to accept Alexander's suggestion and recommend that the Spaniards station a schooner at the mouth of the Ockalagany River to intercept any vessel sent from the Bahamas with trade goods for Bowles.

It was time for Alexander McGillivray to act. He posted a reward of three hundred dollars for Bowles's head, and when there were no takers he dispatched Milfort with three warriors to eliminate Captain Liar.

Milfort returned crestfallen, confessing failure. "Bowles," he said, "seems to have a sixth sense for danger. He seldom emerged from his house while we lay in wait for him, and when he did there were always bodyguards around him. Whom, I might add, he keeps in a constant state of merriment."

Alex was secretly relieved. Murder, though it was common enough in the Creek country, had never appealed to him as an element of diplomacy.

In October, the American John Heth, representing the United States government, arrived in Little Tallassie with $2,900 in gold, the balance due the Creek Nation and Alexander McGillivray by the Treaty of New York. Now thoroughly alarmed by Bowles's machinations, Alexander told the American envoy that war between the Georgians and the Creeks would be the unavoidable result of Bowles's intrigues, unless they were stopped forthwith.

"It's no difficult matter," Alexander said to Heth, "to persuade a few Indians to commit mischief on the frontiers of Georgia. This will give the Georgians an excuse for insisting on further grants, and we will have no choice but to refuse them."

Bowles's promised ship did not arrive. To distract attention from its nonappearance, and hearing that Alexander McGillivray lay ill with rheumatism, Bowles called a meeting of the Lower Creek chiefs. Most of them attended, although the adventurer had made no promises of presents.

Bowles played cannily on the chiefs' old allegiance to the English. He promised to write to the great King and also to Georgia demanding return of the usurped lands and to England asking for aid against the Georgians. He claimed he had six thousand men at his call in the Carribbean to help the Indians in their fight against the Americans.

The Lower Town chiefs not only listened, but broadcast Bowles's message throughout the Nation. Opilth Mico, Alexander's old antagonist, seized the opportunity to declare for Bowles and so did Mad Dog, among others.

"How can the fools listen to the scoundrel!" raged Alex. "The chiefs know that as the possibility of war between Spain and England recedes England has less and less interest in the Indians. And six thousand men—the man is truly a talented liar!"

"Call a meeting of the Lower Creek," advised Milfort. "Speak out against him."

"How can I, ill as I am?"

"Then let Sophia speak for you."

"No," said Alexander definitely. "Bowles would say I used a woman to fight my battles for me."

He felt embittered at Bowles's success. By listening to the turncoat he felt the Creek chiefs had shamed him in his own country. This being true, let them look for someone else to manage their affairs. He was even giving thought to leaving the Nation for treatment of his rheumatism by the Spanish doctors in New Orleans. If in his absence things went from bad to worse, and Bowles continued to solidify his position, the Creeks would have only themselves to blame.

In January, 1792 Bowles switched tactics and moved boldly against William Panton at St. Marks. A group of his men entered his store there and calmly proceeded to take it over. The Spanish garrison at St. Marks was inadequate to the task of dislodging them. Within hours at least a hundred Creeks had made themselves master of the place.

William Cunningham, the Bowles lieutenant who had led the raid, told his prisoners that it was Bowles's ultimate intention to turn the Indians and Spaniards against one another and put the Floridas into confusion so that the people of Kentucky and Cumberland might settle there. He also meant to open the Mississippi to white settlement, and after the Spaniards had been expelled from the country, attempt the conquest of Mexico and Peru!

Yet before either Alexander McGillivray or William Panton had time to take steps against him, Bowles had tumbled from his new heights. Invited to a conference at New Orleans with Baron de Carondelet, who had just replaced Estevan Miró, Bowles went aboard one of the Baron's ships and was promptly and perfidiously arrested. A short time later he was sent to Havana, and from there to Madrid. For five years he was to be a Spanish prisoner.

Bowles's threat to Alexander McGillivray seemed to be over, and there was rejoicing in Little Tallassie. Almost automatically the Beloved Man regained much of the prestige he had lost.

But Alexander did not reckon with the possibility that Carondelet's next move would be against him. In early February of the next year, 1792, Captain Pedro Oliver, a French-born Spanish agent, arrived in Little Tallassie to live there among the Indians.

Oliver's aims were three: to get the Creeks to set aside the Treaty of New York and the marking of the Creek-American boundary, which was to be accomplished by the following spring; to spy upon McGillivray; and to destroy his influence over his people. Failing the last, he was to work towards replacing him with William Augustus Bowles as chief of the Creek Nation.

Any doubts Alexander may have had about Oliver's true purpose were soon dispelled. Oliver immediately claimed that Bowles had shown intercepted letters to Governor Carondelet proving that Alexander secretly favored the Americans.

Alexander smiled. "Have you seen these letters, Captain?" Oliver admitted he had not.

"I can tell you their contents. Bowles must have picked

up some printed matter of the Yazoo and Tennessee companies, who took the liberty of using my name in order to persuade people of property to join their schemes. If my name appeared in these papers without my authority, I can hardly be held responsible for it." He paused. "Tell me, is Captain Liar receiving the good treatment from the Spanish authorities he is accustomed to?"

Oliver muttered that he didn't know. His next move, a few days later, was to threaten his host with the loss of his Spanish pension unless he gave up the one paid to him by the United States. Alexander reminded the captain that the United States pension was in lieu of restitution of his father's estates. If Spain felt it wished to reimburse him for them it was free to do so. Again Oliver retreated in confusion, and Alexander could not avoid the conclusion that he was not a very polished representative of his country's interests.

The Spanish agent was not long in making known his desire to call a Congress of the Creek chiefs, at which he could speak against the Treaty of New York. Alexander's response was that this meeting could be held as soon as possible, but first it would be necessary to find a good Spanish interpreter for Oliver, not an easy task.

"How long do you think this will take?" asked the captain, frowning.

"A month or two," replied Alex.

"Two months!" exclaimed the Spaniard. "Surely you know which white men in the Nation speak Creek and Spanish?"

"They come and they go. I will have to send out messengers to several towns. Perhaps, Captain, you would prefer to find an interpreter yourself?"

Hastily Oliver replied that he would leave that task to his host.

Alexander had no intention of finding an interpreter quickly, nor did he feel he owed Oliver who had come to Little Tallassie to work against him, anything more than courtesy, if that. Moreover he resented the man's arrogance. In the next weeks he sent a procession of "interpreters" to Oliver's quarters, each one more impossible than the last. One could write Spanish but spoke it badly; another spoke Creek but not Spanish. At his wit's end, Oliver stormed into Alexander's house, charging that he was deliberately and maliciously making matters difficult for him.

"But, Captain," Alex said innocently, "this is not my fault, but that of ex-Governor Miró. For years I asked him to station Spanish interpreters in the Creek Nation, but he never thought very well of the suggestion."

"Colonel," fumed the Spaniard, "you will not prevent me from presenting myself to your chiefs. And don't think I won't report your conduct to Madrid!"

"I am sure you have already, judging by the numbers of expresses you have already sent from here. Tell me, Captain, will you not be criticized for the expense when you have managed to say so little?"

He had hit on an exposed nerve. Speechless with rage, Oliver flung out of the room.

By now the Americans, alarmed that a Spanish agent was at Little Tallassie, and that the boundary line had not yet been run, dispatched a new commissioner, James Seagrove, to report on Oliver and see if Alexander McGillivray could be prompted to action.

Alexander had no real desire to see the line run, and was anxious to find some way to postpone indefinitely the settling of boundaries. In this respect at least, the Bowles affair had its use, for as he told Seagrove truthfully, the Lower Creek chiefs still loyal to Bowles would have nothing to do with settling the boundary at this time and would undoubtedly attack the American surveyors who attempted to do so.

The simultaneous presence of Spanish and American agents at Little Tallassie, each with a diametrically opposed purpose, led to a comic opera situation that Alexander could not deny he enjoyed.

Seagrove had hired a brave to spy on Oliver, and Oliver had hired two braves to keep him informed of Seagrove's comings and goings. All three warriors reported finally to Alex.

When Oliver learned that he was under surveillance by Seagrove, he determined to look over the American's papers, and took the opportunity to do so while Seagrove was at one of his many meetings with Alexander. To keep the pot boiling, the latter arranged for the American's spy to break in upon the meeting with news of what Oliver was doing. Racing to his lodge, Seagrove caught the Spanish agent red-handed. Ordering the embarrassed Oliver out of the place, he returned, raging, to the plantation house.

"I demand that Oliver—the skulking thief!—be expelled from the Nation!" he shouted.

"I'm afraid that will be impossible, Commissioner," Alex told him. "I am bound by treaty with Spain to entertain any agents who come to reside here."

"And you are also bound by treaty with the United States to expel any of our enemies on demand!" Seagrove retorted.

"But how do you define your enemies, Commissioner? Is the United States at war with Spain?"

Nonplused, Seagrove ended the conversation.

On Oliver's part, the Spaniard was so humiliated at being caught by Seagrove that he kept to his quarters for almost a week. This made Seagrove chafe at the bit, for he was anxious for Oliver to quit his lodge so that he could pay him back by going through the Spaniard's papers.

Alexander obliged the American by asking Oliver to come to the plantation for a talk. It had hardly begun before the Spaniard's spy interrupted the meeting to say that he had seen Commissioner Seagrove entering Oliver's lodge.

Oliver returned quickly to his quarters, to find Seagrove sitting at his desk. The two men nearly came to blows, and some choice insults were traded. Although the incident had repercussions at New York and in Madrid, Alex found it highly amusing, and Louis Milfort laughed so hard that he fell into a hiccoughing fit.

It took two months before Oliver found an adequate interpreter. Alexander could no longer postpone a council of the chiefs, which was held at Little Tallassie in late May.

The story of Oliver's comic difficulties with Seagrove was known throughout the Creek Nation. Added to this drawback was the fact that Alexander McGillivray could count on the loyalty of all the chiefs present, even those Lower Creek headmen still under the sway of William Bowles, for these chiefs believed that Bowles still detested the Spanish.

Oliver made the further mistake of speaking at excessive length, and before he was through some of the older chiefs were dozing. The Spaniard said that it would be prejudicial to the Creeks to conclude the Treaty of New York, to cede the Oconee lands and to permit the line to run as the Americans had drawn it.

It was to the Creek interest to accept Spanish protection, which offered all necessary assistance to defend their lands and their lives. The Americans, Oliver said, wanted to force them to conclude the New York Treaty. To prevent this they should form an alliance with their brethren the Cherokee, Chickasaw and Choctaw, who would also receive Spanish aid with which to attack the Americans. The new governor of Louisiana offered to hold a meeting in July of the chiefs of the four nations, in which they would treat to conclude a new defensive alliance under the protection of Spain. He requested that the Creek chiefs now give him an assurance they would attend this meeting.

Alexander was caught unawares. In any meeting of the four nations the Creek vote would count only as one of four, and in the event that the other nations voted for Spanish protection in a war against the Americans, the Creek Nation would be hard put to stay neutral in a conflict that would mean the destruction of all the tribes. He must move quickly to prevent a resolution in favor of Oliver's suggestion.

He rose to say that the Treaty of New York had been signed with the approval of Estevan Miró, Baron de Carondelet's predecessor. Baron de Carondelet was evidently in favor of an offensive war against the Americans. Therefore he himself felt that before decisions of any kind were reached, he had better confer with the Baron in New Orleans.

So far as a meeting with the other nations was concerned, he would suggest that it take place not next July but in early September, because of the Creek harvest and festivals held in the summer months.

The murmur of agreement that met his remarks indicated that the Creek chiefs were with their Beloved Man. Oliver hid his disappointment as best he could. He was later to write to Carondelet that "it is obvious that McGillivray's motive is to postpone, and if possible, prevent action of the Creeks against the Americans. His journey to confer with you in New Orleans is but a pretext to this end. There are many signs of his liking for the Americans. Once I came upon him dressed in his American general's uniform. Immediately after my arrival in the Nation he proudly showed me the golden epaulet Washington had given him in New York. Then, indicating a gift that had recently arrived from his father in Scotland, he said, 'This I received from my natural; this'—pointing to the epaulet—'my political and adopted father, Washington.'"

Yet, on July 5, Seagrove wrote to Washington, "I fear General McGillivray is not faithful to the United States; and I have my suspicions that if any mischief is brewing, he is deeply engaged in it. Why else should he journey to New Orleans to meet with the governor of Louisiana?"

Had he been able to read Seagrove's letter, Alex would not have cared. A few weeks before Janine had died of the fever, throwing him into a deep depression that was to last

Baron De Carondelet

for months. He was unconcerned with suspicions, Spanish or American. He was concerned with one thing only—to prevent the Creek Nation from becoming involved in a war with the United States to suit the pleasure of Governor Carondelet, who wanted the Indians to demand that the United States return to the boundaries of 1772, which anyone could see was quite impossible in this much changed world of twenty years later.

Francisco Luis Hector, Baron de Carondelet, was born at Noyelles, Flanders, in 1748. Accompanied by his wife and daughter, he arrived in New Orleans in 1791 to take over the government of Louisiana and West Florida. Devoting himself to public works, he built a canal that gave New Orleans an outlet to the Gulf, reformed the police and instituted a street lighting system in the capital. He worked to better the condition of the slaves, risked his career to protect the commerce of Louisiana against the unwise policy of the Spanish court, labored incessantly to repel the rising tide of the American frontiersmen, and to extend Spain's dominion over the whole of the Mississippi Valley.

He was conscientious, tenacious and brave. And yet he was a poor replacement for Estevan Miró, and his administration was an unfortunate one for his country, for the province and for the Baron himself. His task was one of extreme difficulty, and Carondelet was unfitted for it by either temperament or training. Coming to Louisiana from the governorship of Guatemala, he was completely ignorant of local conditions. He was slow to learn, loath to take the advice of well-informed subordinates and unable to discriminate between the false and true in the many rumors that reached his ears.

In dealing with him, Alexander had two main objectives. He must prevent the Baron from forcing the Creek into an offensive war. Yet a defensive war with the Americans might well prove essential to the Creeks' survival, and against this possibility he must obtain arms and ammunition from the Spaniards, his only source.

Carondelet was a stubborn man; also a ruthless one, as he had demonstrated with Bowles. Alex had no assurance he would leave New Orleans with what he had come for. Moreover he himself could have been in much better health, not only for the demanding negotiations ahead of him, but for the long trip to New Orleans. His rheumatism was bothering him again, along with the sick headaches.

The trip to Mobile by water and again by water to New Orleans depleted his strength so much that, once arrived in the Spanish capital, he took to his bed for several days.

Carondelet sent his personal physician to attend him along with several baskets of fruit and delicacies. Yet the Baron did not call personally and in his messages addressed him as colonel, ignoring his American rank.

This told Alexander something about the governor and his psychology that he had been unable to glean from his correspondence with him or from Captain Oliver. Carondelet could not be as confident as he pretended to be; otherwise he would have felt no need to impress his visitor with his unavailability.

On their first meeting Carondelet, after offering condolences on the death of Alexander's wife, tried to get him on the defensive on the issue of Commissioner Seagrove's presence and activities in the Creek Nation.

Alexander reminded him that by the Treaty of New York, approved by his predecessor, American agents had a right to reside among the Creek. He added, "Of course Seagrove's main purpose is to get a boundary drawn. He has not as yet succeeded."

He pressed on to the issue of Bowles. "Your Excellency, Captain Oliver tells me that William Bowles is receiving excellent treatment in Madrid. I would like to ask why an enemy of Spain and myself should be given a chateau for his personal comfort. Is it possible that you have some future in mind for this man who has attempted to destroy me?"

"I am sure Oliver was exaggerating," Carondelet said, reddening. "Of course we Spaniards are a civilized people, and do not treat our prisoners like cattle."

"Of course," said Alexander ironically.

Carondelet changed the subject to that of the Indian confederation. The Americans, he said, feared that the Indians of the South would ally with those of the North to make war against them, particularly because the latter were enjoying a good deal of success at the moment in the Ohio region. American diplomacy was therefore engaged in turning the southern tribes against one another. President Washington, the Spanish had learned, had sent a representative to the Choctaw Nation promising them territory that belonged to the Creek and the Chickasaw. At the forthcoming meeting of the southern Indians this matter could be discussed and aired. What were the colonel's ideas in general on the subject of an Indian confederation?

"Your Excellency, you know that five years ago there was no stronger advocate than I of a confederation of the southern and northern Indians. The times, however, were not ripe for it. Now, despite the success of the northern Indians, they are no riper, in my opinion. Too much has happened. The Americans, fortified by their constitution, are too strong. American settlements in Kentucky and Tennessee have grown apace. Your own country, you must realistically admit, has been reduced by the French Revolution as a factor in North America. Her prestige has also suffered by her capitulation in the Nootka controversy."

"I do not agree," said Carondelet impatiently. "I believe your pessimistic assessment of Spain's continuing role in North America is the result of your new friendliness towards the Americans. It is quite possible that an Indian demand for a return of the boundaries of 1772 would be met, should the southern Indians threaten an alliance with the northern tribes as the price of it."

Carondelet, Alex thought, dealt in fantasy; moreover he did not know George Washington. The President of the United States was not a man to capitulate to blackmail. Nor did the Spaniard stop to realize that the northern tribes would not take kindly to being used in such a scheme, even granting that a North-South confederation was feasible.

"Your idea is an interesting one, Baron," Alex said tactfully. "I shall give it some thought."

In five days of talks they hammered out an agreement, signed on July 6, 1792, that was precisely what Alexander had hoped to get from Estevan Miró in the 1780's. The Spanish guaranteed all Creek lands beyond the limits formerly granted by the Spanish to the British, and the Creeks were bound to expel all intruders from these lands within the next two months. The Creeks were promised any arms and ammunition needed. A conference of the southern Indians was set for Natchez late in the year, enough time for Alexander to persuade neighboring chiefs that Carondelet's new offensive policies were unrealistic.

In Mobile, on his way back to the Creek Nation, Alexander received a letter from the governor increasing his annual pension by fifteen hundred dollars a year, "in reward for your good services" and informing him that American commissioners to the Choctaws and Chickasaws had been unsuccessful in inviting them to sign a treaty at Cumberland which would have enrolled the Indians as auxiliaries of the United States army in a war against the Northern tribes.

Alexander returned home in early October, weak from a severe fever and gout he had contracted in Mobile. He wrote William Panton: "Every periodical attack grows more severe and longer in continuance. The gout now mounts from my feet to my knees, and I am still confined to the fireside."

But despite pain and illness he kept control of Creek affairs. He coped incessantly with Pedro Oliver, busy inciting the Creek chiefs to the warpath. He met with the chiefs of the Chickasaw at Little Tallassie and gave them a strategy by which they could avoid the building of American forts in Cumberland and Kentucky. He corresponded with both Carondelet and Seagrove, now on the Oconee, persuading the Spaniard against provocative acts, and the American to postpone the running of a line between the Creeks and the Georgians until a settlement more favorable to the Indians than the line desired by the Georgians, should have been reached between the Spaniards and the United States representatives now negotiating in Madrid. Seagrove had also begun to press for the commercial treaty mentioned in the Treaty of New York.

In December, still not fully recovered from his illness, he

attended the general meeting of the four nations called by
Carondelet in New Orleans. The trip so exhausted him that
he could attend only some of the sessions, and his influence
over the proceedings was accordingly diminished. But so
long as negotiations were still going on in Madrid on the
settlement of the Creek-Georgia line, Carondelet could not
forcefully press for a general attack on the American settlers,
and the conference produced little more than talk of eternal
friendship and alliance.

Yet the Spanish governor had decided that overt hostilities
in the Cumberland would not be met with United States
government retaliation, for on Alexander's return to Little
Tallassie, and with the beginning of the New Year, there
was sudden panic in the Cumberland country. Captain John
Linder of Tensaw and other partisans of the Spanish raised
volunteers who attacked the Cumberland settlers. Carondelet
hired two American emissaries to the Cherokee Nation to
incite them to make war on the Cumberlanders. The people
of Cumberland fell victim on all sides, while many settlers
on the Georgia frontiers shared the same fate. Captain Oliver
swaggered about Little Tallassie like a cock of the walk;
Alexander had long since come to detest him.

Seagrove came to Little Tallassie posthaste with a plea
from President Washington that General McGillivray do
what he could to put a curb on the Spaniards. The United
States government knew that although a certain number of
Creeks had taken part in the recent Cumberland raids,
McGillivray himself was not responsible.

The American commissioner was in Little Tallassie for
three days. On the second he received word that a large body
of heavily armed Shawnees had camped at Souwanoga on
the Tallapoosa. It was obvious they were there to wage war
on the Cumberlanders at the Spaniards' behest.

Seagrove came to the plantation house to confront Alexander with the news and demand an explanation. Unfor-

tunately Pedro Oliver was there at the moment. It was the kind of situation that summed up Alexander's predicament and taxed his powers of diplomacy to the limit. He stood in the middle between antagonists both of whom he was allied with and both of whom were intent upon using his people for their own ends. To complicate matters, he had been ignorant of the fact that Carondelet had sent the Shawnees.

He turned to the Spaniard, who was enjoying not only Seagrove's anger but Alex's discomfiture. "On whose authority did the governor send these warriors?" he demanded of Oliver.

"On his own, and by invitation of Wellbanks, Bowles's lieutenant."

Alexander controlled his anger with difficulty. Oliver had forced his hand. If he were to back down now, not only would Oliver gain prestige, but also Wellbanks, and by extension, Bowles. He himself would be revealed to Seagrove, in addition, as being unable to control the infiltration into his Nation of foreign warriors.

Seagrove, Alex noticed, was smiling smugly. It was time to fight this madman Carondelet, and his arrogant flunky Oliver.

Alexander summoned all his reserves of strength. "Captain," he told Oliver coldly, "the Shawnees must leave the Creek Nation by sundown tomorrow. If they do not, I will attack them and expel you."

Although he paled Oliver blustered: "You would not dare to break the treaty. The consequences would be too unpleasant."

"Unpleasant also for you, who have grown so fond of speechmaking to the Creek chiefs, and also of our women. Captain, I await your decision."

Oliver licked his lips. He was much less confident now. "I cannot make such a decision without approval of the governor."

"That would take weeks."

The Spaniard weighed his predicament. The presence of Seagrove made it more difficult; to lose face before the American was intolerable. "I will talk to the Shawnees," he said.

"The decision is yours, not theirs."

Oliver broke. "All right, I will leave for the Tallapoosa immediately," he said, and left the room.

Seagrove laughed admiringly. "General, that was masterly. Although outmaneuvered, you attacked on the flank and routed the enemy!"

But Alex did not feel like a victor. Bathed in perspiration, he had collapsed into his chair. His head was splitting and his leg was on fire. He wondered if the powders Carondelet's doctor had prescribed for him would really do any good.

Ever since the decline of Alexander's health Carondelet had been urging him to come to New Orleans and put himself under the care of his doctor. In early January, 1793 Alex and a small party of warriors left Little Tallassie for the Louisiana capital.

He got no farther than Pensacola. Shortly after his arrival he became ill with a complication of disorders that Governor O'Neill's physician was unable to diagnose. His warriors stood outside William Panton's house, where their chief was staying, their heads bowed in grief. Quinine did not reduce his fever and he soon became delirious. But lucid moments alternated with his ravings, and on February 16 he asked Panton to call O'Neill.

The governor tried to make light of his condition, saying that he had been ill before. Alexander shook his head wearily. "No, this is the end. I wish to make my will. I leave my estate to my children and declare William Panton as their executor and guardian."

On the evening of the seventeenth he seemed to rouse a

bit, and asked for refreshments. But as the night wore on he lost consciousness. Panton called his physician, who could do nothing for the dying man.

Alexander McGillivray died at eleven o'clock that night, far from his beloved banks of the Coosa. He was thirty-six years old. He left his two children, Alexander, Jr. and Elizabeth, and his mother, Sehoy, now a woman of fifty-one.

Burial in the Catholic cemetery of Pensacola was refused him since he was not of the faith; dead, he was spurned by the Spaniards who had courted him so assiduously while he lived. The interment took place in Panton's garden with full Masonic honors. The Indians who had accompanied him on his last journey followed his casket to the graveyard, howling with grief. The whole of the Creek country went into profound mourning, and Alexander McGillivray's people thought bitterly of how he slept, not along the Coosa where he was born, but in the alien "sands of the Seminoles."

When he heard of Alex's death, George Washington wrote Secretary Knox of it, lamenting the passing of a "remarkable man" and their friend. Washington called few men remarkable, and few his friend.

This obituary notice appeared in the August, 1793 issue of the London *Gentlemen's Magazine,* a newspaper whose columns were usually reserved for reports on English royalty and the English great.

> "Feb. 17. At Pensacola, Mr. McGillivray, a Creek chief, very much lamented by those who knew him best. There happened to be at Pensacola a band of Creeks who watched his illness with the most marked anxiety, and when his death was announced to them, and while they followed him to the grave, it is impossible for words to describe the loud screams of real woe which they vented in their unaffected grief. He was by his father's side a Scotchman of the respectable family of Drumnaglas, in Invernesshire. The vigor of his

mind overcame the disadvantages of an education had
in the wilds of America; and he was well acquainted
with all the useful European sciences. His accomplish-
ments as the diplomat of his people are too many and
varied to mention here. It is only since Mr. McGillivray had influence amongst them that his people have
allowed the slaves of a deceased master to live." *

In writing to Lachlan McGillivray of his son's death,
William Panton said,

"Your son was a man that I esteemed greatly. . . . I
found him deserted by the British, without pay, without money, without friends and without property,
saving a few Negroes, and he and his nation threatened with destruction by the Georgians unless they
agree to cede them the better part of their country.
. . . I advised, I supported, I pushed him on to be a
great man. Spaniards and Americans felt his weight,
and this enabled him to haul me after him, so as to
establish this house with more solid privileges than
without him I should have attained . . . What I intended to do for the father I will do for his children.
They have lately lost their mother, so that they have
no friends, poor things, but you and me. My heart
bleeds for them, and what I can I will do. The boy
Aleck is old enough to be sent to Scotland to school,
which I intended to do next year. . . ."

Today Alexander McGillivray's gravesite on West Main
Street in Pensacola is marked by a bronze tablet. Nearby are
the ruined walls of the Panton and Leslie warehouse. He has
one other monument. At the crossroads hamlet of Walls-
burg, Alabama, a granite boulder marks the site where the
Talleyrand of Alabama was born.

---

* From *McGillivray of the Creeks*, by John Walton Caughey. Copyright
1938 by the University of Oklahoma Press.

XII

EPILOGUE

Two months after Alexander McGillivray's death the boundary negotiations being held in Madrid between Spanish and American representatives terminated inconclusively.

All Spain would admit was the probability of her ultimately allowing the northern boundary of her West Florida possessions to be in the line of 32°28'. She was also disposed, though reluctantly, to allow the Americans certain trading privileges in New Orleans, subject to duties. Much ill-feeling was engendered between the United States and Spanish governments, while the people of Georgia were enraged, censuring the federal authorities for the weakness and irresolution displayed in their conduct of the negotiations. They threatened that if the federal government neglected much longer to drive the Spanish from the territory that they claimed they would seize it themselves.

In these disputations Spain assumed unwarrantable grounds. She even opposed the running of the line around the Oconee lands, although nine tenths of this territory lay within the limits of West Florida. Continuing to claim surveillance over Creek affairs by the Treaty of Pensacola, Spain avowed her determination to protect them against the encroachments of the Georgians.

The death of Alexander McGillivray left a vacuum of leadership among the Creeks that was never filled satisfactorily by Spain and William Panton. In 1798, when Spain finally admitted, by the Treaty of San Lorenzo, that Creek territory was outside Florida limits, she abandoned all search for a successor.

The Creeks' attempt to find another Alexander Mc-Gillivray was as fruitless. Louis Milfort was tried and found wanting, whereupon the Frenchman, leaving Jeannet behind, departed for Paris where he remarried and became a general in the army of Napoleon. The White Lieutenant proved no better. Three years later the Creeks accepted as their leader the American agent Benjamin Hawkins, who had negotiated with Alexander ten years before. Hawkins, who remained with the Creeks until the War of 1812, earned their gratitude by his deep devotion to their cause and his improvement of their agriculture and industries. .

But Hawkins never replaced his predecessor. There was no one, in the Creek ranks or out of them who had Alexander McGillivray's education, his subtlety of mind, his consummate diplomacy and his insight into the problems of his people.

Inevitably the "Emperor of the Creeks," in death had his critics. Seagrove charged that it was deceitful for a man to swear allegiance to one country when he still professed loyalty to another. Others said that honors and pay had too much influenced his conduct.

Yet the facts belie both charges. Alexander McGillivray could not afford loyalty either to the United States or to Spain because neither was the disinterested friend of his nation. So he was forced to remain neutral between the two great contesting powers, alternately playing Spain against America and the Americans against the Spaniards, with the survival of the Creek Nation the stakes in his tremendous game.

No Indian patriot could have done differently at that time and in his place, and none could have done as well.

Money never influenced his conduct. For all except two years of his employment by Spain his salary was only fifty dollars a month, and he never asked for more, even though his work involved heavy expenses. He did not desert Spain even when the state of Georgia offered restitution of his family estate on condition that he do so. Washington and Knox were prepared to offer him much more than the annual stipend he agreed to. He neither profited from the land companies that solicited his help, nor from his association with William Panton, whom he made the richest man in America. What he wanted from Panton was not money but favors that would profit the Creeks.

Later historians were kinder in their assessment of the Beloved Man, noting his great achievements. By means of his policy of watchful neutrality, he piloted his people safely through the Revolution, while his less cautious neighbors paid in blood and treasure for their espousal of a losing cause. When, in 1783, with the withdrawal of Britain from the continent, his people stood without a protector, he kept their territories inviolate for as long as possible, while maintaining the Creeks' primacy among their Indian neighbors. In the brief span of nationhood still left to them, his "consummate craft and masterly diplomacy," in the words of Theodore Roosevelt, "enabled the Creeks for a generation to hold their own better than any other native race against the Americans."

"He was," wrote a Georgia historian, "by all odds the foremost man of Indian blood and raising that Anglo-America has ever seen; one who was universally allowed and felt in his day to be the very soul of the Creek Nation, which was almost absolutely swayed by his genius and will.

> "At his death, he was scheming to construct a grand confederacy of the four great southern tribes which might serve as a bulwark to the whole of them against the grasping designs of both the United States and Spain. Had he lived to bring his plan to perfection and launch it into operation, there is no telling how

much it might have changed the whole character and current of our subsequent Indian relations and history and prevented many disastrous Indian, and perhaps also Spanish, events that afterward took place.

"It might even have been that the Creeks, Cherokees, Choctaws and Chickasaws . . . would have become, under his auspices, one grand, consolidated Indian commonwealth, rooted and flourishing permanently on their beloved ancestral soil, and destined finally, perhaps, to full fraternal incorporation into our mighty American system of states."

But fate had decreed a tragic destiny for Alexander McGillivray's people. A few thousand warriors could not be allowed to retain rich hunting ranges coveted by the land-hungry settlers. In 1805 the Chickasaw ceded land in northern Alabama to the United States. A few months later the Cherokee relinquished some of their claims and in the same year the Choctaw ceded five million acres of tribal land, part of which was in southwestern Alabama. However, more than nine-tenths of all the land in the present state of Alabama still remained in Creek hands when the Creek War broke out in 1813.

Two years before, Tecumseh, the great Shawnee chief, had visited the Alabama tribes in an effort to weld the Indians into a league against the Americans. His lieutenant in the Creek country was Josiah Frances, son of a Scotch-Irish trader and a more implacable foe of the Americans than Alexander McGillivray had ever been. Through Spanish emissaries in Pensacola Frances obtained British war supplies, and in the spring of 1813 the Creeks took up the warpath. Their leaders were Charles Weatherford's son, William, better known as Red Eagle; Josiah Frances, Peter McQueen and High Head Jim.

The Creeks won the first skirmish—the Battle of Burnt Corn—and on August 30, 1814, a war party under Weatherford captured and destroyed Fort Mims. But the Creek vic-

tory was short-lived. Andrew Jackson, with Tennessee riflemen and bands of friendly Indians, marched to the upper
Coosa and pushed southward. The Creeks fought bravely,
asking no quarter, but battle after battle went to the lanky,
redheaded general of Tennessee militia. The battles of Talla-
dega and Horseshoe Bend broke the power of the Creek Confederacy forever. Jackson dictated the terms of the peace
treaty by which the Creeks lost all the land west of the Coosa
and were restricted to an area in eastern Alabama.

By 1816 the Cherokee had ceded all their lands to the
Americans except a small area in northeast Alabama. The
Chickasaw gave up all their territory with the exception of
a small tract in the northwest. The Choctaw met a similar
fate.

With three-fourths of the state open for settlement the
whites poured in to take up the rich farmland. In 1830 the
Choctaw gave up, ceded their land at the Treaty of Dancing
Rabbit and moved west of the Mississippi. The Chickasaw
gave up their territory also, and like the Choctaw left to
establish new homes in the West.

But the Creeks, who still held much of their tribal domain,
blocked the way of the incoming settlers from Georgia.
Skirmishes occurred. The United States government, despite
George Washington's pledge of eternal protection to Alexander McGillivray, forced the Creek chiefs, in 1832, to cede
all Creek land and accept removal to the West.

Trouble came when the white settlers jumped Creek
country boundaries before the time fixed by the Treaty of
1832. Bitter controversy arose between the state and national
governments, and United States troops were sent to enforce
terms of the treaty. The matter was finally settled by Francis
Scott Key, sent from Washington as federal representative.

But the Creeks were loath to leave their ancient hunting
grounds, and as more and more settlers pushed into Alabama, they became increasingly restless. Brushes between
the border whites and the Indians were continuous through-

out the summer of 1836. Many Creeks joined the Seminoles of Florida, who, led by Osceola, himself a native of Alabama, were waging desperate war against the United States.

An army of 3,000 Alabamians, reinforced by 1,600 friendly Indians, marched against a band of 700 Creeks. General Winfield Scott arrived in time to stop the impending battle and persuade the Creeks to surrender rather than face certain annihilation. Except for those who had gone to Florida, the Creek allowed themselves to be sent West. By 1839 the Cherokee had been forced to follow.

It was a monstrous affair—a death march complete with manacles, and the sick and the aged dying under soldiers' bayonets. More than a quarter of the Cherokee perished. Many Americans could not believe such things had happened, and to this day history texts in American schools and colleges mention them only in passing. Perhaps our writers of history are ashamed.

Descendants of the Indians who once occupied Alabama now live in Oklahoma, where they still follow agricultural pursuits. Today the Creek, Seminole, Chickasaw, Choctaw and Cherokee are known—the name has its irony—as the "Five Civilized Tribes."

The humbling and removal of the Creek Nation was the final tragedy against which Alexander McGillivray fought so bravely—and hopelessly. But as Theodore Roosevelt wrote, he was "perhaps the only man who could have used aright such a rope of sand as was the Creek Confederacy."

But the Beloved Man was cut off in his youth. It was a bitter blow for the Creek. For, had he lived his normal span, such a man might have used his rope of sand to save his people.

BIBLIOGRAPHY

Adair, James. *The History of the American Indians.* Johnson City, Tennessee: Wautauga Press, 1930.

Alder, John Richard. *The American Revolution.* Boston: Little, Brown & Co., 1954.

Bartram, William. *Travels.* New York: Barnes & Noble, 1940.

Baynton, Benjamin. *Authentic Memoirs of William Augustus Bowles, Esquire.* London, England: Printed for R. Faulder, 1791.

Campbell, Richard. *Historical Sketches of Colonial Florida.* Cleveland: Williams Publishing Co., 1892.

Caughey, John W. *McGillivray of the Creeks.* Norman, Oklahoma: University of Oklahoma Press, 1938.

Chappell, Absalom H. *Miscellanies of Georgia.* Columbus, Georgia: Gilbert Printing Co., 1928.

Crane, Verner W. *The Southern Frontier, 1670–1732.* Ann Arbor, Michigan: University of Michigan Press, 1964.

Foreman, Carolyn T. "Alexander McGillivray, Emperor of the Creeks," *Chronicles of Oklahoma,* VII, 1929.

Hawkins, Benjamin. *A Sketch of the Creek Country in 1798 and 1799.* New York: Bartlett & Welford, 1848.

Milfort, (Leclerc) Louis. *Mémoire ou coup d'oeil rapide sur mes differens voyages et mon séjour dans la nation Crëk.* Paris, 1802.

Millard, Joseph. *The Incredible William Bowles.* New York: Chilton Books, 1966.

Morison, Samuel E. *Oxford History of the American People.* New York: Oxford University Press, 1965.

Nelson, William H. *The American Tory.* New York: Clarenden Press, 1961.

Orrmont, Arthur. *The Amazing Alexander Hamilton.* New York: Julian Messner, 1964.

Pickett, Albert J. *History of Alabama.* Sheffield, Alabama: R. C. Randolph, 1896.

Pope, John. *A Tour Through the Southern and Western Territories of North America.* Richmond, Virginia: John Dickson, 1792.

Romans, Bernard. *A Concise Natural History of East and West Florida.* New York: Pelican Publishing Co., 1961.

Roosevelt, Theodore. *The Winning of the West.* New York: G. P. Putnam's Sons, 1896.

Stokes, Thomas L. *The Savannah.* New York: Rinehart, 1951.

Swan, Caleb. *Position and State of Manners and Arts in the Creek Nation in 1791.* Philadelphia: Longmans Green & Co., 1857.

Van Tyne, Charles H. *The Loyalists of the American Revolution.* New York: Macmillan, 1929.

Whitaker, Arthur P. "Alexander McGillivray," *North Carolina Historical Review,* V, 1928.

Whitaker, Arthur P. *The Spanish-American Frontier, 1783–1895.* Boston: Houghton Mifflin Co., 1927.

Willett, William Marinus. *A Narrative of the Military Actions of Colonel Marinus Willett.* New York: G. & C. & H. Carvill, 1831.